ALANA VALENTINE is a multi-award-winning playwright, director, and librettist. In April 2022 her play *Wayside Bride* opened at Belvoir Theatre and played until May 2022. Having worked with Bangarra Dance Theatre for ten years as dramaturg, in 2022 Alana was the co-writer, with Stephen Page, of *WUDJANG: Not the Past*, music by Steve Francis. At the 2022 Adelaide Festival Alana was the co-librettist, with Christos Tsiolkas, of *WATERSHED: The Death of Dr Duncan*, music by Joe Twist, directed by Neil Armfield. In October 2021 *The Sugar House* was given an acclaimed UK premiere at Finborough Theatre in London and in August 2021 Steamworks productions in Perth remounted a 20 year anniversary production of *Savage Grace* (with the same cast) at the State Theatre of WA. Alana won the 2021 Australian Writers Guild Award for Music Theatre for her libretto *Notre Dame*, was nominated in 2020 for her libretto *Flight Memory* and was also nominated in 2019 for her co-written libretto, with Ursula Yovich, for *Barbara and the Camp Dogs*. *Barbara and the Camp Dogs* also won Helpmann Awards in 2019, including Best Original Score and Best Musical, and 2020 Green Room Awards, including Best Original Score and Best New Australian Work. Alana and Ursula Yovich are working on a screen version of *Barbara and the Camp Dogs* to be produced by Bunya Productions. Her plays are published by Currency Press, including a book about her verbatim/close work practice – *Bowerbird: The art of making theatre drawn from life*. In 2019 the Seymour Centre in Australia presented *Made To Measure*, a commission from the Charles Perkins Centre, University of Sydney, where Alana was Writer in Residence. In September 2022 she collaborated with erth visual and physical theatre on *arc*, which premiered at the Sydney Opera House in late 2022.

Dedicated to Margaret Noffs

Alana Valentine

WAYSIDE Bride

CURRENCY PRESS
The performing arts publisher

CURRENCY PLAYS

First published in 2023
by Currency Press Pty Ltd,
PO Box 2287, Strawberry Hills, NSW, 2012, Australia
enquiries@currency.com.au
www.currency.com.au

Typeset by Lucia Nguyen for Currency Press.
Cover design by Emma Bennetts for Currency Press.
Cover images are used with permission. Clockwise from top: Dawn Munce, Isabella and Hung Tran, Sharon and Ian Day, John and Anne Egan, Nola and Bruce Hogan, Graeme and Philomena South, Maria and Vicky Chandor and Dell Ponnusamy, Patricia and Vernon Lack, Rex and Helen Hewett, Paul and Jennifer Marshall, Jake and Madeline Simcoe, Serge and Ursula Zuffo, Janice Powell.

A catalogue record for this book is available from the National Library of Australia

Contents

Currency Press acknowledges the Traditional Owners of the Country on which we live and work. We pay our respects to all Aboriginal and Torres Strait Islander Elders, past and present.

Sacha Horler and Brandon McClelland in Belvoir Theatre's
Wayside Bride, *2022 (Photo: Brett Boardman)*

Memories of Nan and Pa

'My body, like the clothes I wear, will one day belong to the dust of the centuries but my spirit will continue its journey through time and space.' I recited these words to Nan the night before she dropped her body and continued her own journey through time and space.

'Really darling? Is it true?' she asked me.

My grandfather, Ted, or Pa as I called him, had written and spoken those words often when he was alive. He believed it to be true. Nan, I also knew, believed it to be true.

It was me who originally doubted their veracity.

But over the past decade, spending time with the dying, reading anecdotes of near-death experiences and their commonality, being close to suffering day in and out, I now also believed it.

Nan and Pa lived around the corner from us growing up. We would spend Friday evenings at their house. When Pa was still alive and well, we'd wait for him to get home. When he'd finally arrive, the energy shifted toward his presence. Ted would gather the family together and perform magic tricks. He would convince everyone that he could make chairs (and the person sitting on them) levitate. As kids, our hearts were indeed weightless when Pa was around. Despite coming home clearly exhausted, his presence, his being, filled our heart with love. Just love.

One of my last memories of him while he was still healthy is of standing about two feet away from him. He was slumped in a chair, tired of course, but his eyes were trained on me. My eyes on him. I was waiting for the next magic trick.

The next trick would be a disappearing act. I woke up to the sound of the phone one morning. Dad answered, said almost nothing and quickly put the phone down. 'It's Dad,' he said, grabbing a shirt and running out the door. 'Dad's fallen out of bed.'

What followed was years of slow trauma—for Pa, for his sons, his grandsons, but most of all for Nan. Somehow Nan's spirit never gave up on him. You can still dig up TV archives of Nan confidently telling the camera crews that Ted Noffs would be back at work in no time.

But he wouldn't be.

I'd see thousands upon thousands of letters from children my age come in from schools all over Australia. Nan spent every last dollar trying to keep him at home after that. We'd still go around on Friday nights. The kitchen fluorescent light's low buzz reverberated between Nan's shrieks of joy as she'd laugh at our childish antics. Nan would make us Deb—the ready-made mashed potato in a packet. Or order us a plethora of pizza and a gallon of Coca-Cola.

Nothing appeared too painful for Nan and everything and everyone was accepted and loved as they were. It was difficult to make her angry —and as part of my burgeoning adolescence, I'd certainly try!

Pa was still there until I was 15—well, they said it was Pa. His emaciated body was contorted like a rag doll. He would mumble and sometimes yell. It was difficult to fathom as a child. What happened to my invincible hero? The godlike grandfather who filled me with a sense that anything was possible.

Now I wondered—was there actually a God like Nan and Pa had said? It didn't feel like it anymore.

As I grew older, I'd enjoy meeting Nan's eccentric friends, like one who read my palm and declared to Nan that I'd soon see 'aura'. Nan was quite ethereal herself. She would recount stories of UFOs, ghost stories and past life memories.

As a nan, you would be hard pressed to find a better one. She gave me almost anything I asked for—as her own ageing mother 'Gran Nan' would regularly admonish her: 'You're spoiling him, Marg!'

And yet, though the love filled the air, there was always a pain there too. Some deep regrets. Not that she regretted giving so much to the community but you could sense that if she could go back in time, she may not have allowed Ted to give so much of himself away.

You can give and give and give but there's always a cost. That cost comes in many forms but none greater than the one your family pays when you're gone too soon.

Years later, when I was in my twenties, Nan had moved to Queensland. She would be down on the floor, sorting through boxes of Ted's books and get me to write small notes to give me context for each adventure that lay ahead: 'Kurt Vonnegut: your grandfather's favourite author and pen pal!' 'Dag Hammerstad [Ed: Hammarskjöld? TBC]: Tragic death but a beautiful mind.' 'Rilke: Beautiful German poet.' And so on.

Nan would have admired Alana Valentine's writing.

Alana has brilliantly portrayed the love, the tension and the resilience of Nan and Pa's relationship whilst giving space to the tenderness that gave breath to their community work—to their life's purpose and to the ultimate bond that allowed them to be a creative force behind nation-changing programs from Lifeline to the Freedom Rides, to Wayside Chapel and finally, as Ted began to war with the church, he made preparations in creating the Wayside Foundation—today renamed Ted Noffs Foundation in his honour.

The church hated Pa's sense of family—the Family of Humanity: that no-one in the world is a stranger, that we are all included in the love of the universe. It was too broad a definition of God for the church. They wanted a smaller God. A defined God. A Christian God. An exclusive God.

In this way, the Family of Humanity wasn't just a cute phrase—we were raised in it. Seeing those letters pour in for Pa reminded me that I had brothers and sisters around the known universe. It was expected that we would have a small celebration with Nan and Pa on Christmas Eve because they would be giving their time to feed the homeless on Christmas Day. A tradition that famously continues today.

Nan was a saint and the best Nan a kid could have. Pa was a magician and from another world. He was a hero of the spirit and (almost) unstoppable. However, nothing would have been achieved without his 'Marg' and Alana illustrates that beautifully in *Wayside Bride*.

What seemed unstoppable finally came to a halt in 1995. Pa's passing was a lightning bolt through my adolescence. It filled me with an anger that I continue to attempt to transform today—sometimes successfully, sometimes not. But Pa's energy continues to fill my heart and helps me to continue the work in the present moment, through the rehabs and Street Universities dotted around Australia.

Nan would live well into her nineties and always be there for me in my triumphs and struggles. 'Darling, I think it's time you set up a program in Queensland for the kids with drug problems here.' And we did.

We continue that program's vital vision for a safer Australia today.

And so it is with Ted's words—that after our ongoing work in this life, that in our death we will all 'continue our journey through time and space'.

Nan passed away just before *Wayside Bride* made it to the stage but

I was grateful for all the time I had with her, and that Alana listened to me recounting Nan's best moments. Nan is, after all, the protagonist of *Wayside Bride*. For Pa, it was expected that you grab any time you could with him when he was alive—no matter how exhausted he was—because every moment with him was sacred. Everyone, from those who worked with him to his own family, felt that urgency.

It was as if we knew, somewhere deep down, what was coming.

Matt Noffs
CEO of the Ted Noffs Foundation and
co-founder (with Naomi Noffs) of Street University.

My first memories of Grandpa Ted, were when I was around six years old. I was very close to my Nan (Margaret). She lived around the corner from us, so I would finish school and walk over to spend time with her. We'd sit and watch Jessica Fletcher solve mysteries in *Murder She Wrote* together. Nan would make me a cup of tea. Always lots of milk and sugar. It was delicious.

This was just after Ted suffered a massive stroke that saw him bedridden for eight years. Nurses looked after him at home—so he'd be with us watching TV from bed. He couldn't talk much, and when he did, it didn't make much sense to me. When Nan told him I was there, he would burst into tears. 'Ted. It's your grandson, Rupert,' Nan would say. And he'd respond very slowly: 'I'm … sorry.'

I never fully understood what he meant by 'I'm sorry'.

Even though this tragic thing happened to Pa, there was always a lot of love in Nan's home. He had a lot of good care.

I would play with Pa's wheelchair around the house and even learned how to do a wheelie and stay on two wheels for quite a while.

He had a swing to help him get in and out of the bed. I would often sit on the swing, levering myself up and down whilst chatting to him. Sometimes he would respond and say 'I love you darling'. But it was usually tears, and then, 'I'm sorry'.

I remember his large, warm forehead. His pointy nose. His skinny frame. Thin arms. Almost skeletal face. And his perfect, white dentures in a glass of water next to his bed. I still see videos of him and his smile, and remember those teeth ... in a glass of water.

He'd snore with his eyes open. Nan would tell me he always did that.

Pa was later transferred to The Scottish Hospital as his health was declining, and so every Friday night I would drive with Nan to visit him.

Nan would stop by the local corner shop before we arrived, and buy some caramel fudge. It was the most delicious thing I'd ever tasted.

I still remember the smell of the hospital as we walked in. The beeping sounds, the bright lights.

Pa would be yelling out 'Help! Help!' whenever we walked in. He would repeat that, over and over, until Nan and I walked into the room.

Nan would then say, 'Ted, darling. Rupert your grandson is here to see you.' Then the cries would start and 'I'm sorry, darling'.

Sometimes, I would get quite overwhelmed as I didn't know why he would say 'I'm sorry' to me ... so I would walk around the halls of The Scottish Hospital. Just go have a break and so Nan could chat to him. I remember the looks on the patients' faces as I walked past. The families visiting them.

I made a friend at The Scottish Hospital and I often think about her. Mrs Gwen Simpson was her name. She was in the room next door to Pa. I would see her name written above her bed and giggle, thinking about Marge Simpson from *The Simpsons*. She had the most elegant long fingers and perfectly painted pink nails. Her family lived interstate so she didn't have a lot of guests. She always told me there was a can of Coke in her fridge that I could have, and let me eat her M&M's. Thinking about it now, I guess they were always for me.

Recently—actually it was the last conversation I had with Nan—I mentioned Mrs Simpson, and Nan didn't remembered her. Which was odd. Nan remembered everything till the very end, even in her late nineties ... but she told me she didn't remember Mrs Simpson.

Mrs Simpson would tell me how special my grandfather was and how he was 'very famous', which I laughed at. She said how it was a shame he was sick and not to worry. Mrs Simpson once told me how lucky I was to have a grandfather like Ted and even though he couldn't talk to me, he loved me very much.

A few years later, my high school choir group visited The Scottish Hospital and we sang for everyone in the lunch room.

I remember always seeing Mrs Simpson and Pa at the very back of the group. Pa in his wheelchair. His head slightly tilted. His big forehead. I could see him crying as I sang.

It's then I fell in love with singing.

Mrs Simpson was right. I am lucky to have Ted as my grandpa. All the incredible people I've met through him. The guests that now dine at my restaurant or see me perform. The thousands of couples he married or christened. If only we were able to have more time with each other. If only he looked after himself.

I performed in a cabaret space in Ettalong last week, called The Naughty Noodle, which is a safe space for queer people. But not just for queer people. It's a safe, inclusive space that reminds me of what Ted created in Kings Cross. An older, English man came up to me at the end of my performance and said, 'The only reason I'm here is because your grandpa, Ted, married my wife and she's now no longer with us.' I gave him a hug and told him how special it was to meet him and thanked him for coming along. I asked him what Ted was like—as I love hearing stories from people who knew Pa before his stroke. He told me how kind Pa was to them, how 'cheeky' he was. He told me they weren't supposed to get married, but Ted did it anyway. I love that. That was Pa.

Ted's legacy lives on through these stories from people he met. This story by Alana is one of them.

I was asked to narrate a documentary produced by the ABC a few years ago. I went to the ABC studios, sat in the sound booth, and watched the incredible footage of Ted and sixties Kings Cross. The beatniks, bohemians, the down-and-out, politicians, gays, rich, poor, blacks, bikies, the musicians, all in one room under the chapel. People would sing and pray and meditate. Pa would stand in front of a large group of people and call it 'Question Time'. He'd try and answer their questions. They'd debate. Argue. But it was always a safe, inclusive space.

It was very theatrical.

Something else struck me when I saw this footage of Pa. I saw this chubby man walking down the streets of Kings Cross in the late seventies. That forehead I know so well. Those teeth! He was carrying a large box of paperwork and folders. His ill-fitting suit, with flares. The kipper tie. I could see he wasn't healthy. He looked tired.

It made me immediately cry, remembering his voice. 'I'm sorry, darling. I'm sorry.' And the stomach-churning 'Help!' in the hospital hallways.

It put it into some perspective.

What Pa and Nan were doing was revolutionary. I think most of us know that. Especially if you were there and saw first hand. Ted was constantly fighting. Trying to change minds. Change laws. Raise funds for people in need.

Ultimately it did take a toll on his health.

I'm grateful for being asked to share my memories of Nan and Pa for this book. I loved Alana's play. Seeing part of Nan and Pa's story portrayed on stage. They would have loved it too.

Even though my memories aren't the happiest of times, they are memories full of love.

I may not have been able to have a proper conversation with Pa as I grew up, but I look back and realise what he did.

He made a sacrifice.

From an early age, Ted and Margaret devoted their lives to making sure thousands of people across Australia had someone to talk to, had a warm blanket, and had a roof over their head.

Especially the kids—and that was something greater than just this kid.

Rupert Noffs
Owner, The Lucky Bee

A note from the Wayside

To best know where you are heading, it is wise to know where you have been...

We met up outside the Belvoir, the current mob of Wayside team members, consisting of volunteers, staff, visitors and donors. All united in our excitement and love for the impact that Wayside has had on not only our lives, but also on society. We booked out the theatre for the performance of *Wayside Bride*, and from the moment it began until it ended, every seat was only used for its edges as we were transported back to the place where we began.

Wayside Chapel has always been a place of love, acceptance and diversity and to see Alana Valentine's rendering of our history portrayed with humour and honesty was to reconnect us with our founding, a legacy of love that continues to this day and will do so, we hope, well into a future we know nothing of, except that it requires that same love that flowed in 1964.

The play was a stark reminder that Wayside Chapel's legacy comes from the 'gutter up' rather than the 'university down'. From the moment our doors opened we were overwhelmed by people who had been shunned by society and had nowhere else to turn. People facing isolation and addiction finally had somewhere to seek acceptance and support. When members of the Aboriginal community approached Wayside speaking of racism in the sixties, the Freedom Rides, led by Charles Perkins, soon left from our doorsteps to tour through small regional towns in New South Wales, as a peaceful protest against discrimination. When heroin hit the streets and people were passing out or worse nearby, the Tolerance Room opened at Wayside and eventually led to the first medically-supervised injecting centre. When everything began shutting down two years ago when the pandemic kicked off, we not only stayed open but hit the streets, taking all our love and care to where it was most needed.

Anyone can be very busy running an ambulance service at the bottom of a cliff and you will get a lot of adulation for doing so, but the moment you stop and head to the top of the cliff to ask why people are falling off it in the first place you cause a commotion and get accused of being an iconoclast. Everyone who has held a leadership position here has been accused of disrupting what appears to be 'the normal order of events', and our city is better off for it.

Ted Noffs is known as the founder, but *Wayside Bride* shows how pivotal a role his wife Margaret Noffs played in establishing the small chapel on a side street in Kings Cross as one of our nation's best-known centres of love.

The play is also a reminder of how our gift to history is not just our care of those who fall through the cracks. In the sixties and seventies, Wayside confronted the limitations of marriage norms. Nowadays, it no longer means much to join together a Catholic and a Protestant, or someone who has been divorced, but it wasn't all that long ago that it was a cultural taboo that we snubbed our noses at. Love is love and its litmus test is 'does it build us up and weave our hearts closer together?' Couples desperate to marry but unable to do so in every other church flocked to Wayside in the early days to declare their love in our little Kings Cross chapel. Couples no longer face the hurdles of yesteryear, but I'm pleased to say they still flock to Wayside to marry because they believe in our mission of creating community with 'no us and them'.

I recently conducted a wedding, which, if we counted, would likely be the 50,000th one conducted by Wayside Chapel. To be a minister at the Wayside is to have the regular privilege of conducting and celebrating weddings. All of them are precious, unique and a celebration of the joy that life can bring, often in the most unexpected of ways.

We all left the theatre deeply moved by Alana's story and how the course of her life has been touched and directed by a little chapel on a side street off the main road. It is a story about weddings, but it is about so much more, about how institutions can stifle life rather than promote love. About how one little place can be a sustained protest against the way society constitutes itself, and how, in the words of Arundhati Roy, we can be a part of another world, one that 'is not only possible, she is on her way. On a quiet day, I can hear her breathing'.

Thank you Alana!

Jon Owen
Pastor and CEO of The Wayside Chapel

Writer's Note

Matt Noffs contacted me during rehearsals to let me know about the passing of his grandmother, Margaret Noffs, Ted Noff's wife. She died in December 2021 at 95 years old, and was apparently lucid to the end. When I told the cast of the play there was a collective exclamation of grief, a deep understanding that this was the passing of a great Australian, a compassionate, extraordinary person who, no less than Ted, was responsible for the establishment of the remarkable Wayside Chapel. We had been rehearsing with the line, 'Margaret Noffs is still alive' for so long, but now she was gone.

A brochure called *The Wayside Chapel, The Biggest Little Church in the World* claims that between 1964 and 1986 Ted married twenty-four thousand couples from one hundred and thirty-two different nations. My own mother, Janice Powell was among those married at the Chapel and was the inspiration for this work. One of the great delights of conducting interviews from this play has been the continuing radicalism of the people who were married at Wayside – the sense that by defying religious convention at one of the most important moments of their life, their marriage, they continued to carry with them a general scepticism about institutions and authority. One of the pains, of course, is that I interviewed and heard from many more people than I could possibly put in my play. To those whose incredible stories I had to leave out, please accept my apology.

Matt Noffs told me that almost every day of his life, strangers who hear that his surname is Noffs will ask if he is related to Ted and then say quickly that their brother, father, uncle, sister-in-law etc were married by Ted. That has been my experience too in working on this play. It's the thing I love most about being a playwright who draws their work from living testimony — it is the experience of hitting a rich seam of memory and pride and pain that is connected specifically to this city of Sydney but, I hope, says something unique about the flavour of religious radicalism when it is expressed in an Australian context.

In Mike Willesee's 'This is Your Life' TV program about Ted Noffs there is a parade of astonishing visionaries who embrace him, among them Charles Perkins, the nation-changing First Nations activist who says of Ted Noffs, 'I suppose he's probably one of the greatest living Australians and he made a man out of me, he made me see good things in people'. The two embrace warmly as they discuss the Wayside Chapel's breakfast program for Aboriginal children.

Thank you to Karen Rogers, Ben Winspear, Lee Lewis, the City of Sydney, Graham Long, Louise Gough, Sue Donnelly, Aaron Beach, Eamon Flack, Hannah Goodwin, Wendy Howell, Vicki Gordon and this astonishing cast and creative team. Thank you to all at the present Wayside Chapel for their support and love (it's what you continue to do). I hope that whether you are of the generation who knew and admired Ted Noffs for his heretical stances, who know that a family member or cherished friend were married there, or are a young person who just needs to believe that change is possible, you will find sincere hope in this play, genuine belief in the legacy and vision for a society that cares for its vulnerable and leaves no-one behind. Ted was a great smiler, a great laugher, a big cryer as were so many of my interviewees....so please feel free to be copious in your response to the work of this amazing cast.

Margaret Noffs, I dedicate this play to you.

Alana Valentine
April 2022

Thank you to:

Development: Ben Winspear, Lee Lewis, and Karen Rogers.

Workshop actors: Meyne Wyatt, Bishanyia Vincent, Tony Phelan, Lynette Curran, Sonia Todd, Gareth Davies, Terese Tate Britten, Celia Ireland, Steve Rogers, Mandy McElhinney, Ella Prince, Josh Price, and Sarah Meacham.

Interviewees: Paul Stacy, Tom Kelly, Sally Dolman, Mike and Rosie Sprange, Lorraine (and Graham) Tredinnick, Isabella Tran, Claire and Peter Calahan, Berwyn Lewis, Noreen and Peter Solomon, Vernon and Patricia Lack, Sean and Joan Smyth, Ursula Zuffo, Rev Bill Crews, Jacquiline Smith OAM, Patricia Small, Christine Rijks, and Peter Utting.

Website submissions, publicity and admin assistance: Bede. S Pearsall, Kate Cocker, Abby De Borde, Cate Richards, Bob Chandler, Nola and Bruce Hogan, Allan James Grey, Helen Claire Hewett, Ross and Christine Bowen, Caitlin Allen, Nicki Packer, Fiona Murray, Sharon Day, Marie Healy, Annette Herman, Vicki Jones, Marita Nieuwenhuis, Valerie Jones, Pamela Springate, Maxwell Charles McKeown, Eveline Molines, Dr Sandra Symons, Jane Elspeth Scott, Betty Hutton, Graeme and Philomena South, Fay Briggs, Paula Noakes, Dawn Munce, Janice Isobel Edmunds, Leslie Forman and Iris Joan Beringer, Michael Maude, Rene Louise Egan, Harriet McDonald, Perryn Louise Ryan, Louise Searle, Fiona Fuller, Madeline Simcoe, Jenny Aitkins, Tania Lee Turbin, Margaret and John Malins, Pamela Lanskey Williams, Linda Jacoby, Jenny Taylor, Michael Far, Coral Graham, Brendan Hynes, Jennifer Marshall, Jacki Mison, Bill Code, Jonathan Coleman, Ita Buttrose, Allan, Fay, June, Shane, Dean, Cynthia Stericker, Cris MacDonald, Dr Lisa Murray, Eimear Elkington, Timothy Atlee- Bowra, Simon Marnie, Graham Long, Wesley Enoch, Vicki Gordon, Jon Owen, Matt Noffs, Bryce A Wastney, Sharne McGee, Maxine Schellhorn, Simone Whetton, Carolyne Johnstone, Renee Krosch, Michael McGuirk, Claire Grady, Kathie Turton, Olga Nowicka, Helen Grasswill, Jennifer Trinca, Madeline Parker, Guy Cooper, Wendy Howell, Dom Mercer, Mary Walsh, Kath Davis, Catherine Skipper, Andrew Collis, Pamela Briggs, Heather Robinson, Aaron Beach, Amy Goodhew, Aishlinn McCarthy, Glen Richardson, Tim Kliendenst, Belinda Dyer, Linda Morris, Janine Huan, Louise Gough, Vyvyan Nickels, Rosie Baker, Belinda Kent, Lou's Place participants who wish to remain anonymous, Kerry Roman, Alistair Hill-Lees, Rebecca at Noffs Foundation, Roy Powell, Cynthia Colli, Annette Herman, Brendan Hynes, Will and Ashleigh, and Kate Hunter.

Wayside Bride was first produced by Belvoir Theatre, Gadigal country, Sydney, on 2 April 2022, with the following cast:

JANICE/MARGARET	Sacha Horler
ALANA	Emily Goddard
TED NOFFS	Brandon McClelland
ORSON / ISABELLA / 2021 MARGARET	Maggie Blinco
JOSEPHINE / MIRIAM / JOANNE	Angeline Penrith
SEAN / MICHAEL / BRAND / CHARLIE	Marco Chiappi
URSULA / ROSIE / DUSTY / IRMA	Rebecca Massey
JOAN / SHARNA / CLAIRE	Sandy Greenwood
CLYDE / PAUL / SAILOR	Arkia Ashraf
MIKE / BILL CREWS / JON OWEN	Rashidi Edward

UNDERSTUDIES / STANDBYS
Ákos Armont, Merridy Eastman, Abbie-Lee Lewis, Matilda Ridgway, Christopher Stollery, Contessa Treffone, Charles Wu

Directors, Eamon Flack and Hannah Goodwin
Assistant Director, Matilda Ridgway
Set Designer, Michael Hankin
Costume Designer, Ella Butler
Costume Design Associate, Nell Ferguson
Set Design Associate, Keerthi Subramanyam
Lighting Designer, Damien Cooper
Sound Designer and Composer, Alyx Dennison
Sound Design Mentor, Steve Francis
Choreographer, Elle Evangelista
Fight Director, Nigel Poulton
Vocal Coach, Danielle Roffe
Andrew Cameron Fellow, Abbie-Lee Lewis
Stage Manager, Cecilia Nelson
Assistant Stage Managers, Amelida Grindrod and Alexandra Loguidice

CHARACTERS

JANICE/MARGARET, female, 40-70 years old.

ALANA, female, 30-50 years old.

TED NOFFS/IAN, male, 40-60 years old.

ORSON/ISABELLA/2021 MARGARET, female, 40-70 years old.

JOSEPHINE/MIRIAM/JOANNE, female, 40-60 years old.

SEAN/MICHAEL/BRAND, male, 40-70 years old.

URSULA/ROSIE/DUSTY/IRMA, female, 40-70 years old.

JOAN/SHARNA/CLAIRE, female, 30-50 years old.

CLYDE/PAUL/CHARLIE/SAILOR, male, 40-60 years old.

MIKE/BILL CREWS/JON OWEN, male, 30-50 years old.

Non-binary persons may be cast, as preferred.

PROLOGUE

ANGELINE: Twenty-twenty-two (or current date), early evening. This is Gadigal land on Eora country.

SANDY: Nineteen-seventy-five, early morning. This is Gadigal land on Eora country.

ANGELINE: Past, present, future. This is Gadigal land on Eora country.

SANDY: We begin today by acknowledging the sacred custodianship of this land by First Nations people.

ANGELINE: This was, is and always will be Aboriginal land.

SANDY: And at three am in the morning, when a playwright crawls out of a warm bed and begins to type …

ANGELINE: She is working and dreaming and creating on Aboriginal land.

ACT ONE

SCENE ONE

ALANA *is present (and may be writing or typing) when* JANICE *enters.*

JANICE: So now I get my turn.

ALANA: Sorry it's taken me a while to get to you.

JANICE: You're a busy girl.

ALANA: Yeah, well, a lot of people have responded to the project.

JANICE: That's what you wanted, isn't it?

ALANA: Sure.

JANICE: So stop complaining.

ALANA: I'm not complaining. I'm just saying that's why it's taken me a while.

JANICE: Just as well I'm a patient woman.

> *Pause.*

ALANA: There have been some great stories so far.

JANICE: Well that's good then, isn't it?

ALANA: There was this woman Valerie Jones who told me that they used a pink cement mixer to take the bride and groom from the Wayside Chapel to a home in Lindfield for the reception.

JANICE: Couldn't afford a hire car.

ALANA: She said that it was reported in the evening paper but she could never find proof.

JANICE: Probably never happened.

ALANA: Why do you say that?

JANICE: Makes for a good story so who needs the truth.

ALANA: But she's telling me the truth.

JANICE: She could be making it up.

ALANA: I don't think she is.

Pause.

Anyway I'll see if I can find it in the papers from the time.

JANICE: You do that. Though, you're not a real historian so ...

ALANA: So?

JANICE: So it doesn't really matter, does it?

Pause.

ALANA: Reverend Graham Long told me that he conducted a service where everyone thought a drug dealer was marrying a policewoman but they weren't really being legally married because it would affect her job status so they just had the ceremony and never signed the paper.

JANICE: He couldn't do that.

ALANA: Well he said he did.

JANICE: What? He told you that he lied to the wedding guests?

ALANA: It's not a lie. Or if it is, it's one the couple wanted him to tell.

JANICE: It was a fraud.

ALANA: They just didn't sign the paper so it wasn't legal, but it's hardly fraud. It was a commitment in front of their friends.

JANICE: We were married, legally married, by Ted Noffs.

ALANA: Yes, so were most of the people I've spoken to.

JANICE: He married a lot of people.

ALANA: About twenty-five thousand. Sometimes every half an hour on a Friday/Saturday.

JANICE: I know. I was there.

ALANA: I spoke to a guy in South Africa, by phone, who was the verger at nine-hundred-and-twenty-three weddings.

JANICE: Right.

ALANA: Anyway, enough of other people.

JANICE: Other people's lurid tales. I don't have anything like that.

ALANA: I'm not looking for lurid.

JANICE: Well it sounds like you're looking for unusual, for interesting at least.

ALANA: I get to decide what's interesting.

JANICE: Yes. Well. Let's get this over with then.

Pause.

ALANA: Of course, if this is still a good time?

JANICE: I was just doing some sewing, so this is a good break.

ALANA: What are you making?

JANICE: Oh, just some carry bags for the shopping.

ALANA: Not a nice dress for yourself?

JANICE: I don't go anywhere to wear a nice dress.

ALANA: You were married in nineteen-seventy-five?

JANICE: February.

ALANA: And you wore a mustard Chanel suit with silver buttons.

JANICE: Faux Chanel. I made it myself from a Butterick paper pattern.

ALANA: It looks like Chanel in the photos.

JANICE: Well that was the idea.

ALANA: So why the Wayside Chapel?

JANICE: It was around the corner from where Roy was staying.

ALANA: Okay. But you knew of Ted Noffs and the work of the Wayside Chapel?

JANICE: Sort of. Neither of us were religious.

ALANA: But you wanted a church wedding?

JANICE: Not really. It was as good a place as any.

ALANA: But Ted put a few noses out of joint. Did you like that about him?

JANICE: No. It was really just because Roy was staying around the corner. In a hostel for new migrants. Ten pound poms anyway.

ALANA: Right. Ted's willingness to marry divorcees was part of it?

JANICE: Well, I was divorced, so yes, that meant he would marry us. But it wasn't really part of it the way you're trying to make out.

ALANA: I'm not trying to ...

JANICE: It was just around the corner so it was convenient. I'm sorry if that doesn't make for some terrific story about Ted's politics or my politics or my commitment to radical social change or whatever else it is you want me to say.

Pause.

ALANA: Please don't be like this, Mum.

JANICE: Like what?

ALANA: I'm not asking leading questions. I'm trying to draw you out.

JANICE: Yeah, well, there must be thousands, tens of thousands of people married at Wayside who can't explain why they went there. What are you going to do with that?

ALANA: I don't know. I don't know alright.

Beat.

I have all these stories and I'm trying to work out what links them.

JANICE: What does link them?

ALANA: You.

JANICE: I was just one in a long line. I'm not any kind of link to anyone else.

ALANA: No, you're a link to me.

JANICE: Why does it need to be about you?

ALANA: ...

Pause.

JANICE: Do you have your own memories of the day? You were there.

ALANA: I don't remember anything at all actually. I think I remember the little white handbag I was carrying.

JANICE: Yeah well, you loved that handbag.

ALANA: What happened to it?

JANICE: You left it in the back lane where we were living and someone stole it.

ALANA: We were living above a fruit shop.

JANICE: Our landlord was going broke because the supermarket had started carrying fruit and veg. They closed on Saturday afternoon and dumped all their veg in a skip. Roy used to say to me, Janice, think of that skip as our veggie patch.

ALANA: I was a dumpster diver from way back.

JANICE: Little scavenger. Finding something among the scraps.

Pause.

ALANA: I know I was at both your weddings. In the belly for number one and flower girl for number two.

JANICE: You're not going to put that in, are you?

ALANA: Why not?

JANICE: People don't want to hear about that, Alana. In fact, don't feel obliged to put any of this in. Just because I'm your mother, I don't want special treatment.

Pause.

ALANA: Did he ever try to see us?

JANICE: Who?

ALANA: My father.

JANICE: Roy?

ALANA: My biological father.

JANICE: No he did not.

ALANA: But ... he didn't wonder. How we turned out?

JANICE: Men like that don't wonder, they just scarper.

ALANA: But even basic human curiosity would make you want to know what a child grew into.

JANICE: Well he didn't. Not a card, not a letter, not a phone call. He put you out of his mind. Because he did not love you.

ALANA: Mum.

JANICE: I know that's harsh but it's the truth. He no longer loved me and you were a summer hat to chuck out el pronto.

ALANA *allows this to land on her.*

ALANA: Because you were divorced you were an outsider, back then. Socially.

JANICE: There's no need to be rude.

ALANA: You felt excluded in some way.

JANICE: I am not going to talk about this now.

ALANA: Then when?

JANICE: You can't understand unless you were there.

ALANA: But you can tell me.

JANICE: I can't tell you. No-one can tell you because it's not about information. It's about something else.

ALANA: What?

JANICE: Suffering. You can't understand unless you have suffered.

ALANA: Everyone has suffered.

JANICE: Don't give me the crock of shit you feed your theatre luvvies. Your mother Janice was married there, so what. Biology doesn't give you perception. Sentiment doesn't give you insight. It's never going to be understood by someone who thinks the world shines out of her glitter-encrusted vagina.

ALANA: At least you didn't say cunt.

JANICE: I meant to say cunt.

ALANA: Or did you mean to say lesbian?

Pause.

JANICE *doesn't answer. She crosses her arms and takes a moment to speak.*

JANICE: Before Ted was going to marry you, he called you in for a bit of an interview. And I'm not very good at interviews.

ALANA: There's some devastating self-awareness.

JANICE: So I needed something to give me confidence.

A black sixties dress with gold rik rak around the collar and cuffs magically appears and hovers above the action.

ALANA: What this?

JANICE: Perhaps you could recycle it.

ALANA: You mean upcycle?

JANICE: No I mean recycle. I had to go in for an interview and this is what I made, to wear in there.

ALANA: Because the more vulnerable you are, the more you dress up.

JANICE: You should try it.

ALANA *touches the rik rak trim along the dress.*

See the pleats on the side and the the rik rak running dead straight along the trim. That's hard to do. So when I put it on, I touched those pleats and I felt that trim and I thought they're hard to do, but I did them. In this dress, none of the rules of the normal world apply. It's as if suddenly life has thrown the switch to neon.

JANICE *looks up and the stage lights go to neon.*

There was a homeless woman on the street, under the magnolia tree. And she was always just ranting away to herself.

JANICE *exits.*

During ORSON*'s speech* ALANA *looks at the dress, smells it and suddenly she is wearing it. She wears a wig, or a seventies hairband.*

TED *enters and sits beside them as* ORSON *speaks. Orson becomes increasingly troubled as the speech progresses. Ted holds their hand.*

ORSON: [*whispering*] I bring the tree
I bring the tree
buds branches leaves limbs
[*Loudly, becoming increasingly troubled*] Hey Hey!
the Magnolia bay
Bull bay tree
I bring the tree
Grandiflora
Red seed falling
Cables of skin dangling shadows jangling should have been
Padded mat of glossy colour mess of furry pods clotted oyster in my belly,
long cord warm cord plaited with dreams an eel, a wheel,
the feel of he part of me, under the tree.

The shadows and noise are scrubbed away
Under the old Magnolia Bay I lift the creamy flowers
I stroke the leather leaves
Swish swish velvet hurts, it burns, it hurts with pain
The spirit torn into strips
TED: Orson.
ORSON: Ted.
TED: That's right.
ORSON: Orson.
TED: That's right.

ORSON: Now what?

TED: Dunno. Now what?

ORSON: Don't tell me.

TED: No chance, Orson.

ORSON: Don't fix me.

TED: Not a chance.

> ORSON *begins to keen and rock, their arms folded.*

ORSON: Don't fix me. Don't fix me.

TED: No-one's going to fix you Orson. It's alright.

> ORSON *looks at* TED.

ORSON: Are you going to fix me?

TED: No.

ORSON: Why not?

TED: I don't know how to fix you.

ORSON: I see. I hear.

TED: Do you?

ORSON: You too?

TED: Not really. Sort of.

ORSON: They'll try to fix you.

TED: Will you stop them?

ORSON: What?

TED: Will you help me if they try to fix me?

ORSON: Me?

TED: Yeah.

ORSON: I can't fix anyone.

TED: Me either.

> *Pause.*

ORSON: Now what?

TED: Dunno.

ORSON: Where are you going?

TED: Nowhere. I'm just standing here with you.

ORSON: Then what?

TED: Then I'll go inside if you're okay.

ORSON: The spirit is folded and hanging in the tree.

TED: Yeah, we don't really go in for that religious stuff so much, Orson.

TED *moves as if to leave.*

ORSON: I bring the tree.

TED: You come up for a cup of coffee Orson. If you like, or not, if you don't.

ORSON *sees* ALANA *and speaks to her, as she moves in the corner.*
TED *exits the opposite way.*

ORSON: The flowers brown and bruised on the ground.

SCENE TWO

MARGARET *enters.* JOSEPHINE *and* PAUL *are either onstage or nearby in the audience, and* MARGARET *nods to them as she greets them.*

MARGARET: Good morning Orson. Josephine. Paul haven't seen you for a while.

She sees ALANA.

Hello. How you going?

ALANA *gives a small squeal of shock.*

ALANA: You're Ted's wife.

MARGARET: Only for twenty-four years.

ALANA: You're Margaret Noffs.

MARGARET: Marg. Would you like a cup of tea?

ALANA: That'd be great.

MARGARET *goes to make the tea.* ALANA *looks at* JOSEPHINE *on the other side of the stage and tentatively nods hello. She looks back at* ORSON *who shouts at her.*

ORSON: Currawong call. Currawong call. I bring the tree.

MARGARET *comes back on with a cup of tea.*

MARGARET: You must be Janice.

ALANA: Janice?

MARGARET: There's an appointment for Janice. Divorced, two kids.

ALANA: And a fiancé /who lives nearby.

MARGARET: /Who lives nearby. Will he be joining us?

ALANA: No. In fact I'm not/

MARGARET: [*whispering conspiratorially*] We just need him to turn up for the ceremony, right?

> *They laugh.*

ALANA: You do a lot of weddings?

MARGARET: Only about sixty a week.

ALANA: Not so many then.

> *They laugh.*

MARGARET: If you're a Catholic wanting to marry a Protestant. Or a Buddhist wanting to marry a Jew, Ted is basically the only show in town.

ALANA: He's a trendsetter then.

MARGARET: Oh yes. The Family of Humanity. Ted says we're all part of it.

ALANA: You'd have a quieter day if you made the club a little more exclusive.

MARGARET: That's true but who wants a quiet day when you can have the Family of Humanity.

> TED *enters.*

TED: Who are we marrying today, Marg?

MARGARET: Five weddings, three pre-wedding chats. Noreen and Peter Solomon.

TED: Yes. Both atheists but her mother wants a church wedding.

MARGARET: Patricia and Duncan Small.

TED: Raised Methodists but no close family in Australia. I told them we'd give them nothing but good vibes.

MARGARET: And how did they like that?

TED: They didn't know what I meant, but they're back so they must have liked the vibes after all.

MARGARET: You also promised to tape record the wedding for his mother who is in England, so don't forget to mention her in the service.

TED: Isn't it the mother's birthday?

MARGARET: Right. Berwyn Lewis who is a lapsed Catholic woman with a Jewish father marrying a non-observant Jewish man, and Sandra Ross marrying an S. Wiggins.

TED: That'll be Skull Wiggins.

MARGARET: And you're pre-wedding meeting with Sean and Joan Smyth and Ursula McCallum and her fiancé Carol Zuffo.

> *Beat.*

Carol is also a male name.

TED: Yes, there was a King Carol of Romania.

> *Beat.*

I would also marry her to a Miss Carol Zuffo.

MARGARET: I know you would.

TED: It doesn't have the force of law but that's not always the point.

MARGARET: Speaking of the force of law.

TED: What?

MARGARET: Ursula McCallum's first husband was a bigamist.

TED: Okay. So she needs to find out who he was married to in the first place, and get a judge to rule that her marriage is invalid.

MARGARET: So it's not the same as the divorcees you remarry?

TED: No, in this case she was never legally married. And she has to prove that.

MARGARET: Okay.

TED: Anything else?

> MARGARET *holds out a letter.*

What is it?

MARGARET: It's from the New South Wales Methodist Conference.

TED: What do they want? Another affirmation of faith?

MARGARET: A what?

TED: You're supposed to stand up at the Methodist Conclave or whatever they call it and guarantee that you are doctrinally pure.

MARGARET: That doesn't sound like you.

TED: Which is why I never go.

MARGARET: Ted.

TED: I send Clyde along. He can deal with that bullshit.

MARGARET: With compliance to the doctrines of the church?

TED: Yeah. Like I said, he can deal with that bullshit.

MARGARET: Well I don't think Clyde has dealt with it this time.

TED: What?

MARGARET: Read it.

TED: You read it and tell me.

MARGARET: I don't understand it.

TED: The general gist.

Pause.

MARGARET: I think that they're charging you with being a heretic.

He takes the letter and reads it.

And?

TED: They're charging me with being a heretic.

MARGARET: They don't use the word.

TED: They don't use the word eradicate either but that's what it will do to this place. No weddings, no baptisms. Closed.

TED is shocked, the colour draining from his face.

MARGARET: Ted?

Still TED can't speak. MARGARET goes to him and they both exit.

SCENE THREE

ALANA *begins to exit.*

JOSEPHINE: Nah, don't leave.

ALANA: I'm just waiting to see the Reverend.

JOSEPHINE: Ted. You want to call him Ted or he'll have you.

ALANA: Did Ted marry you?

JOSEPHINE: Yeah, there's a story.

ALANA: Hit me.

JOSEPHINE: You mean, tell you?

ALANA: Sure.

Pause.

JOSEPHINE: You had it rough too?

ALANA *tentatively nods her head.*

Two kids uh?

ALANA *sits down, imitating, for a moment, her mother, Janice.*

ALANA: Shotgun on the girl, nailgun on the boy.

JOSEPHINE: Nailgun? As in second one?

ALANA: Second child, nail in the coffin of the relationship.

They laugh.

You?

JOSEPHINE: Two boys, and Shantelle. What mother doesn't want a little girl, you know? Especially if you've had the boys first you crave for the little girl. Every woman except my mother that is.

ALANA: I'm sure she wanted you.

JOSEPHINE: No. No. No. People say to me what would you do if you met your mother and I say, I'd slap her right across the face. That woman denied my existence and shoved me in as a ward of the state. She just hightailed it out of the hospital, left me in the crib.

ALANA: I'm sorry to hear that.

JOSEPHINE: What's your name then?

Beat.

ALANA: Janice.

JOSEPHINE: I'm Josephine.

ALANA: When were you married, Josephine?

JOSEPHINE: The day Nige got out of jail. I was up there, in the crisis centre waiting for him. If I asked them once I asked them a thousand times, where was he? He'd been released that morning so where was he? I was up and down the stairs, confused. Jan, I was that confused. I was more confused than a hungry baby in a topless bar.

ALANA: Funny.

JOSEPHINE: As useless as a one-armed trapeze artist with an itchy arse.

ALANA: Go on.

JOSEPHINE: So Ted's got this really posh wedding going on downstairs. Society lot. Someone who thinks their shit smells better than the rest of us. Nah, they weren't like that but I'm telling the story so let's stick their nose in the air a little for the effect. So Nige arrives. And the man is wearing an excuse for shorts. Is he what! This man, I'll tell you Jan, this man has an arse that is all beer, and no foam, you know what I mean. Lost his shirt somewhere between the big house and this one but he's still got his shorts on.

ALANA: But not for long if you can help it.

JOSEPHINE: Marriage certificate sister you better believe it.

They laugh.

So I asks the crisis counsellor can Nige have a bath in the bathroom. Crisis centre, eh, they've got a bath for crisis cleaning. Right. And they say yes and then what they don't see is me crawl under where the counter is, you got it?

ALANA: I got it.

JOSEPHINE: They don't see me sneak under the counter and go in the bathroom with him. You got it?

ALANA: I think you got it, Josephine.

JOSEPHINE: You're not wrong, Jan. You're not wrong and I have to tell you, I think we might have made a little bit of noise.

ALANA: I suppose there was a bit of knocking and a bit of sloshing.

JOSEPHINE: My sister there was a bit of knocking and a bit of sloshing.

ALANA: Don't tell me that water started pouring down into the Chapel?

JOSEPHINE: It did not. There was no spillage.

ALANA: So it was waterproof?

JOSEPHINE: Waterproof. But not soundproof.

ALANA: Oh.

JOSEPHINE: We hadn't seen each other. I wanted him to know I was pleased he was out.

ALANA: Or in. Or in and out.

JOSEPHINE: Ahhh!

ALANA: And he was pleased.

JOSEPHINE: He was pleased, I was pleased. Only Ted wasn't pleased.

ALANA: No.

JOSEPHINE: No. When he's finished Ted comes boltin' upstairs. Face like a squeezed tea bag. He was that ... He was ... I never seen Ted like that. He was ...

ALANA: Livid.

JOSEPHINE: Livered that's the one. His liver was up. Full as a rain gauge and ready to blow.

ALANA: Didn't like the wedding march you played.

JOSEPHINE: Not one bit. So Nige looks at him and fast as a hell can scorch a feather he says, 'You wouldn't have a go at a bloke for a poke on his wedding day would you Ted?' And that stopped Ted and he said, 'Since when is it your wedding day, Nigel?' and Nige said, 'Soon as you agree to perform the service, Rev.' And that's as true as the king has an egg in his pouch.

ALANA: So you got married in your bath towel?

JOSEPHINE: No. They found me a dress. Half a dress. Didn't want to cover me pins.

She gives a little twirl, wearing the dress that was found for her.

ALANA: Well that's one way to jump the queue.

JOSEPHINE: You want to be my certificate sister you better try something Janice, or I'm telling you, you could be waiting a while.

JANICE: I should go.

JOSEPHINE: Stay here, see if you fit.

JOSEPHINE *exits.*

SCENE FOUR

SEAN *enters and pushes buttons on the onstage jukebox.* ALANA *is standing and* URSULA *is seated nearby.*

ALANA: Hi.

SEAN: Hello.

ALANA: I'm waiting for Ted. To meet with Ted.

SEAN: I'd better join the queue then.

ALANA: You here to see him?

SEAN: Yeah, and my fiancé, Joan. She'll be along in a moment.

ALANA: My fiancé is Roy. And I'm Janice.

SEAN: Pleased to meet you Janice, I'm Sean.

ALANA: You live around here?

SEAN *sits down with* ALANA.

SEAN: Used to. Back in the sixties that was the start of me being a bit homeless, you know. I was one of those young fellas who was full of excitement. And yeah, I was a bit wild and I got into trouble with the police. But the Cross back then was a lot different than it is now. We knew all sorts of people from the television people, criminals, artistic type people. You could walk down the street and it might take you a couple of hours to get from one end of Macleay Street to the other because you always knew somebody on the way. Girls of the night, soldiers, sailors. Tourists, from overseas. You could walk up near the fountain with a can or a bottle in your hand and nobody would say anything.

ALANA: Not these days.

URSULA: There was a lady who lived across near the fountain and she had the first operation, the first transgender operation. She was a very well-known hairdresser in the Cross and her name was Sandy.

SEAN: I was never into the drug scene you see. I used to drink a lot. I think most people, they'd smoke pot if anything. The cops were corrupt. Especially the detectives. I knew a couple of them. Bumper Farrell, he was notorious. Reckoned he was going to clean up the bad elements in the Cross. Didn't happen Bumper. Didn't happen mate. And what was his name ... Ray Kelly ... everybody knew he was a crooked cop. They used to drive up and down the Cross. Hang out the window. Stare at you. And they used to hate the bodgies, if you remember what they were like. Bit like John Travolta in *Grease*. Had that look. So I was one of those. One thing led to another and I done a little stint in Long Bay Jail, I broke into a shop and received stolen goods. Anyway, I come out of jail and I'd met a deaf fella in there and he told me how to speak it a bit and I'd also joined the deaf and dumb society club in the city. I got a bit friendly with some of them. And I just happened to mention to them one day, 'Do you know any girls'. Because I hadn't long been out of jail, see and he said 'Oh yeah, I know some.' So we went over there and she came out ... So I asked her if she would like to go out with me. And she said, 'Well you don't bite, do ya?' We went to this ... I had a suit on. We might have went to some sort of a ball because she worked for Bebarfalds in the city. It was a department store and I think they were having their annual end of year event. But then we went to drive-ins, went to pubs, we used to go out on Sunday ... because no pubs would be open on Sunday so we used to have to go out past the thirty mile limit I think towards Penrith and you could go out there and drink. So we used to go out there on Sundays. Have a few drinks out there when the Rex was closed.

URSULA *leans forward and interrupts.*

URSULA: My mother works as a barmaid at the Rex Hotel. Johnny O'Keefe goes to the Rex to drink because he's really friendly with Mum.

SEAN: I've heard about some well-known people who'd got married at Wayside. Jane Wyman I think.

URSULA: Jane Powell.

SEAN: Jane Powell of course. And Mary Ann Kennerley. I had a look at the place and I'd seen it before because I'd lived up near here of course. So that's where we've decided to get married. Why not. We'll have a friend of ours and his wife as witnesses. Yeah, there'll just be the four of us there. Joan hasn't kept in contact with her family because of the way they treated me I suppose. Joan was born in England and when my family found out they were Irish Catholic and they'd adopted me, see. So when they found out I was marrying an English Protestant they disowned me.

ALANA: Maybe they'll come round.

SEAN: They disowned their first born son and he wasn't even adopted like me. He married a Baptist. They swear they won't speak to or see neither of us till the day we die.

ALANA: How can you disown someone?

SEAN: People do it all the time.

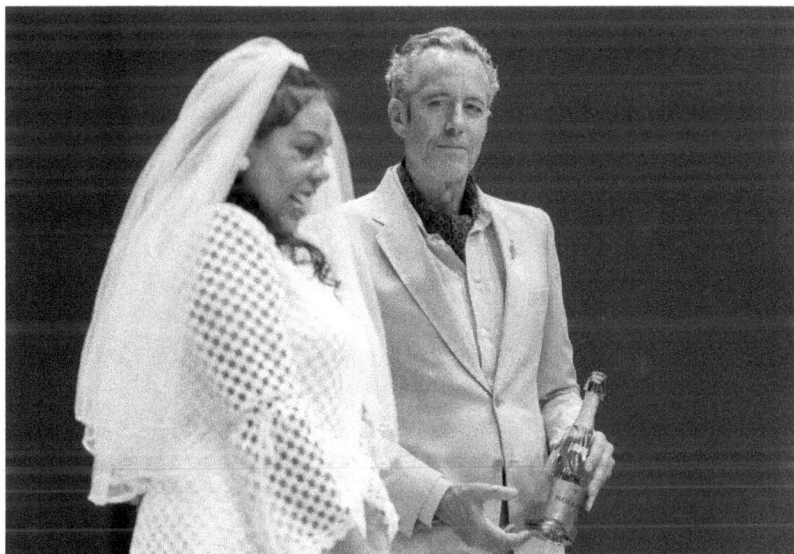

Angeline Penrith and Marco Chiappi in Belvoir Theatre's Wayside Bride, *2022 (Photo: Brett Boardman)*

SCENE FIVE

TED *is sitting, dejected.* MARGARET *enters.*

MARGARET: Not to bother you, Ted, but Miriam is here early.
TED: Miriam who?
MARGARET: Miriam Davies.

> *Beat.*

Who you're marrying at three o'clock.
TED: I won't be a moment.
MARGARET: There's no rush.

> *Beat.*

Only she's in tears.
TED: Who?
MARGARET: Miriam.
TED: It's a wedding. People cry.
MARGARET: They do. The thing is ... she's in tears and she's saying she can't walk down the aisle.
TED: I just can't believe they could be so petty.
MARGARET: Who?
TED: Brand.
MARGARET: The head of the Conference?
TED: President.
MARGARET: And Reverend Brand is the one saying that you're a heretic?
TED: No, Marg, keep up. There's a young Minister, John Hall, who has only been ordained for two years, full of piss and vinegar. He's never heard me preach but he is offended by the very idea of Wayside. So he writes a letter of complaint about me to the Methodist Conference.
MARGARET: You've had letters of complaint before.
TED: Yes, but this time instead of throwing his letter in the bin, they grab it with both hands and say, aha, a patsy with evidence. We can use him to destroy the Noffs and their crazy experiment in Kings Cross.
MARGARET: What evidence?
TED: He drove down and picked up some pamphlets. Apparently you gave him some of my poetry pamphlets.
MARGARET: Me?

TED: Do you remember a bloke, a Minister, asking for some of our pamphlets?

MARGARET: People ask for pamphlets all the time.

TED: Ministers.

MARGARET: Well I can't tell if they're Ministers.

TED: He would have had a dog collar on.

MARGARET: You don't wear a dog collar.

TED: Yes but I'm not your usual Minister.

MARGARET: No Ted, keep up, you're a heretic.

Pause.

TED: Think carefully. Could there have been a Minister asking for some of our pamphlets?

MARGARET: You're going to have to talk to Miriam now, Ted. She's crying and she's refusing to walk down the aisle at three. She's a beautiful girl and we found her a beautiful dress. She looks lovely but she's on her own and the nerves have set in. There's a lot of people depending on you right now, Ted. So I'm sorry that stupid pamphlet-distributing me have got you into some hot water, but right now I need you to come and deal with Miriam.

TED: Tired of the pads in Cairo
Tired of the push in Rome
He peddled pills on a movie-set desert
Sold Whispers out of his zone.

MARGARET: That's in pamphlet that they're objecting to?

TED: I called it 'Prodigal in the Pigsty.'

MARGARET: So you can call the next one 'Calming the butterflies'.

TED: It's not the pamphlet. That's not why they're doing this.

They rush off.

SCENE SIX

SEAN *and* ALANA *are sitting with* URSULA.

URSULA: Do you know the El Rocco?

ALANA: No.

URSULA: You don't know the El Rocco? Everyone knows the El Rocco.

ALANA: Is it a club?

URSULA: Jazz club. Tiny. We had a one room apartment above it. And that's where we lived. So when he came back he had to climb up the awnings across the roof and he got back in through the window.

ALANA: Who?

URSULA: My husband. Or so I thought.

ALANA: Why didn't he come in through the front door?

URSULA: I wouldn't open the door to him. He was a bigamist. The police called him a prolific bigamist. I was one of a dozen women he'd married. Here and in Canada. Prolific.

ALANA: How'd you find out?

URSULA: I opened his mail and he had a group certificate in a different name. And he just admitted it. He said, 'Oh well, you've found out, I've married you under false pretences.'

ALANA: And Ted married you to him?

URSULA: No, not Ted. Ted checks you out before you can get married. He may look like he's very open, and he is, but he's also very shrewd. People think he's a straight line because he's got his suit and tie but he's the same.

ALANA: What do you mean?

URSULA: I mean Ted is sort of ultra-visionary really. When I told Margaret that the man I married when I was nineteen was a bigamist she told me I needed the paperwork to prove it. So luckily my new man, my fiancé, Carol, he was Italian and he knew some people. And we found, a detective not me, he actually found the original wife, who lived in Redfern and she had to come along to court and declare that yes that photo was him and show her own marriage certificate. Because hers was the only valid certificate because you can only marry once. All the rest of us were just mugs.

She laughs.

Anyway she verified that it was him and the judge declared that I was never married and so we took her out to lunch!

ALANA: You were lucky you found her.

URSULA: So this bigamist, La Brock, he was my first husband. Still I found him out and then I threw him out. And then when he climbed back in, will I tell you what he did?

ALANA: What?

URSULA: He grabbed a knife out of the cutlery drawer. I think he was only going to try and scare me ... I don't really think he was going to ... I think wanted me to keep my mouth shut. I don't honestly think he ... it's still frightening when someone gets a knife out to you but I don't think he was going to ... I wouldn't have thought, looking back on it, he would have killed me. He was panicking that I would sort of go to the police which I did ... eventually ... not right at that moment. I was shocked but then I never did anything about it because that was when I was nineteen and now I'm older and I have been so untrustworthy. I mean, he took me out to dinner, place called Sweethearts. More than a coffee lounge, you can get nice meals there. And I was most impressed because I couldn't afford those things. I was an usherette at the Prince Edward Theatre, it's been pulled down now, very beautiful theatre. So I couldn't afford to go out for dinner. People who live in the area just assume that the locals can patronise all the places around here but half the people who live in this area can't afford to go to the restaurants. They just walk past and look at who's in there and dream.

ALANA: But everyone's welcome here.

URSULA: [*reluctantly*] Yeah.

ALANA: No?

URSULA: Yeah, 'course. And you're doubly welcome if you're getting married. Just don't forget whose place it is.

SCENE SEVEN

MIRIAM, *in a full bridal gown and veil, howls loudly as she walks past* URSULA *and* ALANA. TED *enters and sits with her. He does not try to comfort or console her with a touch or anything. He simply sits with her.*

TED: Miriam.

> MIRIAM *is crying, howling, snotty, messy, sniffing, bawling.*

I know.
It's awful.
Whatever it is just let it out.
That'a girl.
You let it all out.

I know.
I really do know.
Right this moment I could cry just like that myself.
I really could.
I could howl like a dog.
I could bawl like a baby.
Because the pain is so deep.
So so deep and awful.
Like a knife plunged deep in your heart.
I know.
I really do know.
So you let it out, Miriam.
I'm not here to hurry you up.
And I'm not here to tell you to get over it.
I don't want you to get over it.
I think it's terrible, whatever it is for you.
It's terrible and you should just cry your heart out.

MIRIAM *stops crying and begins to calm down.*

MIRIAM: I always thought it would be my dad, you know.
TED: What would be your dad?
MIRIAM: I always dreamed my dad would walk me down the aisle.
TED: You did.

MIRIAM *begins to cry again.*

MIRIAM: And I can't go down the aisle by myself.
TED: I know.
MIRIAM: It's too awful. Walking down the aisle by myself.
TED: It's too awful.
MIRIAM: But it is.

Pause.

TED: What if I got Marg to walk down with you?
MIRIAM: No.
TED: No?
MIRIAM: It's not the same.
TED: It's not the same, but is it better than walking down on your own?
MIRIAM: No!

TED: Okay.

MIRIAM: That would be worse.

TED: So it has to be your dad.

MIRIAM: But it can't be my dad. He's refused to come.

TED: I know.

MIRIAM: Which is why I'm crying.

TED: I know. So what do you want to do?

MARGARET *enters, looking stressed.*

Do you want to leave it to another day?

MIRIAM: [*howling*] No!!

TED: Okay.

MARGARET: Only the party for the Lewis wedding are starting to arrive and the Solomons are in half an hour after that.

MIRIAM: You schedule a wedding every half an hour?

MARGARET: Sometimes.

MIRIAM: Why?

MARGARET: If you're Greek Orthodox wanting to marry a Lutheran, or a Hindu marrying a Baptist, or if you want to be in and out like a fiddler's elbow ...

TED: I'm the only Minister who will marry you and have it recognised by the State.

MIRIAM: I'm sorry for holding you up.

Pause.

TED: What's he like?

MIRIAM: Who? Dad?

TED: Yeah. Tell me about him.

MIRIAM: He's tall. I mean, he's taller than me. And he's always very carefully dressed. I mean, not poncy. But he's dapper, you know.

TED: Particular.

MIRIAM: Proud. Handsome. He has a sense of ceremony, a sense that you should rise to meet life.

TED: That looking after yourself means that you're reminding yourself how precious life is.

MIRIAM: Yeah. That's it.

TED: He sounds like a very special man.

MIRIAM: He is.

Beat.

Is there someone other than Marg? I mean someone else?

TED: Like your dad?

MIRIAM: Yeah.

TED: Someone who could stand in for him?

MIRIAM: Yeah.

TED: Just to walk you down the aisle?

Beat.

Can you give us a minute?

TED *and* MARGARET *pull off to the side.*

Find someone.

MARGARET: Who?

TED: Tall, carefully dressed. How about one of the guests from the Wiggins' wedding?

MARGARET: The Wiggins are bikers.

TED: Someone on the street then.

MARGARET: No-one on this street is carefully dressed.

TED: Go round to the Quarter Deck.

MARGARET: To the bar?

TED: One of the men there will be perfect.

MARGARET: One of the homosexuals?

TED: Yes. Tall, well-dressed. Particular. They'll be brilliant.

MARGARET: But they're camps.

TED: Well I'm not asking them to marry her, just walk her down the aisle.

MARGARET: I can't go into the Quarter Deck and ask a homosexual to play Dad.

TED: I'm sure they get asked to do it all the time.

MARGARET: This is not going to do anything for your heretic reputation, you know.

TED: Do you want every bride today to be disappointed?

MARGARET: Can you knock over a pre-wedding meeting first?

TED *says nothing.*

MARGARET *goes over to* SEAN.

Sean and Janice? Janice?

ALANA: Yes.

MARGARET: You can go in.

ALANA: We're not together.

MARGARET: Go in. This may be your only chance today.

SCENE EIGHT

TED *arranges chairs for a pre-wedding meeting with* SEAN *and* ALANA.

TED: You're Sean.

SEAN: That's me.

TED: And Janice?

ALANA: Yes, but I'm marrying Roy and he's marrying Joan.

TED: But neither of them are here.

SEAN: Margaret said you were having a busy day so she thought we should ...

TED: Kill two birds ...

SEAN: Something like that.

ALANA: A bit unorthodox.

TED: Oh, that's us for sure. A pre-wedding chat just to make sure everything is okay for both of you to marry other people who aren't here.

SEAN: Right.

TED: So when you proposed to Joan, how'd you do that?

SEAN: I didn't go down on one knee.

TED: No knee?

SEAN: No, but she wouldn't want that. That's not us.

TED: No fanfare. No Irish dancers jumping up and down all in a line.

SEAN: No.

TED: So how?

SEAN: No, I just said, 'We should get married.'

TED: And she agreed.

SEAN: She did.

TED: Smooth.

> JOAN *enters.*

Here she is. I was just hearing about Sean's proposal.

JOAN: Who are you?

ALANA: I'm Janice.

JOAN: You're marrying Janice now?

TED: No, not at all. It's a busy day, we're having pre-wedding chats ...
as a group.

ALANA: —

TED: Sean was just telling us about his proposal.

SEAN: Her father hates me so I wasn't sure she would marry me.

JOAN: Yes, you were. You knew I'd agree out of spite.

They laugh.

SEAN: Her father's a Cockney and a Freemason.

TED: So an Irish Catholic is his first choice.

They all laugh again.

SEAN: We're talking about a man who, when I drove Joan home one
night, points at me with a twenty-two rifle.

TED: That is a dangerous firearm.

SEAN: If it hadn't been for her brother behind the water tank he probably
would have shot me.

JOAN: No.

SEAN: No?

JOAN: No, he definitely would have shot you.

SEAN: The hatred between the Catholics and the Protestants, the hatred.
I tell you. Before I went out with Joan I went to pick up this girl and
this girl's father meets me at the door and I walk up to the door, all
done up in me good strides and he says, 'If your name is Sean, and
you're a Catholic, you should piss off right now and don't come
back here or else.'

TED: Listen Sean, the only marriage advice I'm going to give you is this.
Never mention the name of any girl before Joan.

SEAN: And is that one of the sacraments of marriage?

TED: No, mate, that's one married man to another. Trust me, you'll
thank me.

JOAN: I'm not the jealous type, Ted.

TED: Jealous, possessive or begrudging, the thing you don't ever do is
give your rival a name.

SEAN: What about kids?

TED: Well, what about kids?

SEAN: I don't want to get married in a Catholic Church but I'd like to see my kids raised Catholic.

TED: And how are you with that, Joan?

JOAN: Depends what you mean by Catholic. You mean go to Mass, be an altar boy seven days a week, and have fantastic sex before marriage?

SEAN: Steady on.

JOAN: What?

SEAN: She's not saying we've had sex before marriage, Ted.

TED: Isn't that what you are saying, Joan?

JOAN: Would you be shocked by that, Ted?

SEAN: What are you doing?

JOAN: I'm asking.

SEAN: She's not. We'd never discuss sex with a priest.

JOAN: He's not a priest. He's married himself. And presumably that means he has sex.

TED: I do have three beautiful sons.

JOAN: That's alright Ted, the one thing you don't have to explain to a Catholic is how you get children.

TED: And you don't have to prove to me that you haven't had sex before marriage.

SEAN: You sure?

TED: Even my Roman tradition brethren would agree that is extremely rare.

JOAN: Try physically impossible.

She nudges ALANA *and they laugh.*

SEAN: See what I'm marrying into, Ted? Now that is what you call English humour.

TED: Which you love.

SEAN: God help me but I do.

TED: Then I can't see any reason not to proceed with the wedding. It'll be short and sweet, but I can book you in, name your date.

SEAN *and* JOAN *look at each other and kiss.*

SEAN: First cab available I reckon.

JOAN: Soon as possible he means.

SEAN: Can you do it today?

TED: Schedule's full today, can you come back?

SEAN: Yeah.

TED: Where you living?

SEAN: We don't mind. We sleep in the back of the car.

TED: What?

SEAN: Yeah, I promised her we'd go travelling. If we get some work we might graduate up to a tent.

TED: And if it's not me, there'll be someone to do it.

JOAN: What do you mean, if it's not you?

TED: Oh, it's nothing. But I thought I should mention it. They're charging me with heresy but I'll fight it. They can't get rid of me that easily.

JOAN: But if the charge sticks, will they replace you?

TED: Actually they're more likely to shut the place down altogether.

JOAN: But they can't do that can they?

TED: Absolutely. They own the building. I'm just an employee. And if I break the contract of my employment, as it were, they can fire me.

JOAN: I thought Ministers were different.

TED: You mean because we're called, vocationally, because it's about faith?

JOAN: Yeah.

TED: Nah. Not so much.

> *Pause.*

JOAN: Then, let's do it today.

TED: Today is a bride called Miriam, among others. And I'd better get back to her. Refusing to walk down the aisle without her dad.

JOAN: If she says no, we'll take the place.

TED: Deal.

> JOAN *and* SEAN *exit.*

ALANA: Why are they charging you with heresy?

TED: I guess we've got time for one spin.

ALANA: Of what?

> TED *wheels on a large bingo wheel. On it are marked various theological questions: 'Virgin Birth', 'Resurrection', 'The Question of Suffering', 'Bad things to good people', 'Homosexuality', 'Divorce', 'Dominion over the animals', 'Women in Ministry', 'Historical evidence of Jesus', 'Do angels exist', 'The second coming', 'The Bible and Slavery', 'Original Sin'.*

TED: Let's play theology bingo. How much attention did you pay at Sunday school?

ALANA: Didn't go.

TED: Well let's see what you've picked up anyway. You game?

ALANA: I don't understand.

TED: The church is so bad at explaining itself that people come up here with questions.

ALANA: About what?

TED: About everything on this wheel. And more. I've tried Thursday night debates, I've tried Sunday morning sermons. But I've boiled it down to this, I can give everyone one spin of the wheel and tell you how my theology differs from that of the Methodist Church. If you can find the one place we agree you get to call bingo and win a prize. Which is one of my books.

He shows her one of his books, secreted behind the Theology Bingo wheel.

ALANA: Do you have to spin or can you just choose?

TED: It's more fun to spin.

She spins the wheel. Whatever it lands on she moves it back to homosexuality.

Excellent choice because it's a nice quick answer and that is that there is no difference and it's not a sin to be who you are.

ALANA: You do know that it's a crime. You can be jailed for it.

TED: Homosexual people are part of the body of Christ and are completely equal, end of discussion.

ALANA: So you are a heretic.

TED: My answer to every question on this board makes me a heretic, Janice. I just don't have the time to let you count the ways. Still want me to marry you?

ALANA: Yes please.

TED: [*calling as he exits*] Welcome to the Family of Humanity.

SCENE NINE

ROSIE *and* MIKE *enter at a pace, holding a bottle of champagne.* ROSIE *goes to* ALANA *and hugs her, hard.*

ROSIE: Hello!

ALANA: Do I know you?

ROSIE: No. But you can't do what's expected of you. Can you?

ALANA: Ah ...

ROSIE: Of course you can't. You have to be original.

MIKE: And rebellious.

ROSIE: You have to question.

ALANA: Question what?

ROSIE: Everything!

ALANA: Okay.

ROSIE: When we got married it was one of the first weddings Ted did outdoors.

MIKE: In a garden. In Wahroonga.

ROSIE: He was late.

MIKE: I forget what his fee was but I think it was fifteen dollars.

ROSIE: Tiny.

MIKE: It was tiny but we still had trouble scraping it together. I remember having it in an envelope and catching him as he was leaving down the side of the house and almost rather furtively handing it to him.

ROSIE: We got married for my parents.

MIKE: We didn't tell them that Rosie was already pregnant.

ROSIE: But it was going to become obvious soon enough.

MIKE: Quite a few of our friends said 'Why the hell are you getting married?' you know.

ROSIE: Because in those days we knew quite a lot of people who just had kids and didn't bother.

MIKE: But the way Ted managed the service, he made us feel like it was something really significant.

ROSIE: Mind you it wasn't like the extravagant weddings you get today.

MIKE: We had a friend in the theatre who organised the food and grog for the whole reception for seventy dollars.

ROSIE: Doris Fitton who was at that stage running the Independent

Theatre came and she knew that it was in a garden and she was wearing gumboots, funny little plastic covers over her shoes because it was going to be in a garden.

MIKE: She knew Rosie was pregnant so she said something to me like 'Are you happy about the baby?' Something very direct. I mean what am I going to say at my wedding reception?

ROSIE: I wore this purple velvet dress.

MIKE: Isn't she beautiful?

ROSIE: And I can still get into it!

ALANA: Even better.

ROSIE: I'm an actress you know, and we had Doreen Warburton there, and Judi Farr was one of our witnesses.

MIKE: Ted wore a light brown, might have been double-breasted, tweedy sort of suit with a waistcoat.

ALANA: So quite formal.

MIKE: We all filed into the house to sign the register and get the certificate and I was intrigued to know that he was Theodore Delwin Noffs. Rosemary's dad was a witness. And then we all went outside again and he said in a big voice, 'And now I want to introduce you to the newly-married couple'. I remember being very moved when he said that. And then he stayed and had a sherry.

ROSIE: Johnny Whitton was there, he was the stage manager at the Independent Theatre and he was very determinedly gay. The theatre was one of the only places you could be determinedly gay. But there were quite a lot of people from the Independent Theatre there. I'd been working there recently.

MIKE: I often think of Ted when we go to weddings now and you hear the priest making gross assumptions about people's religious beliefs in order to try and impose them onto them somehow. Whenever we go to weddings now Rosie listens for the 'love, honour and obey' and at a recent wedding we went to it was 'love, honour and submit'. There was me, Rosie and one other person nearby who all went, 'aagh ...'

ALANA: Was there anyone who objected to Wayside or the opposite, were impressed that you had chosen Wayside?

ROSIE: I mean my family were just happy that I was getting married. At all.

MIKE: In the circumstances.

ROSIE: No, not just in the circumstances. That's how it was in those days, it was 'thank God she's getting married'. We had been living together and that was a bit risqué. But I was an actress so, I went there.

MIKE: It's hard to communicate now just how much social disapproval mattered.

ROSIE: And how much it mattered to us to flout it!

MIKE: Yes!

ROSIE: You're a theatre goer?

ALANA: Me? Yes.

ROSIE: Are you sure?

MIKE: It's not mandatory, Rosie.

ALANA: The truth is, I'm sort of undercover in my own play.

> ROSIE *looks confused and then realises.*

ROSIE: She's a device!

MIKE: She's here to meet Ted.

ROSIE: But now she's done that and she's still hanging around.

MIKE: You can do that here.

ROSIE: She's breaking the rules.

MIKE: She's writing about a man of God.

ROSIE: Theatre goers can handle a big adult conversation about God without choking on their champagne.

> *Pause.*

Risk it.

MIKE: We've got your back.

> *They laugh and exit.*

SCENE TEN

ISABELLA *enters. She is like a ghostly apparition in a long white gown, in the style of a Vietnamese ao dai.*

ALANA: Are you real?

ISABELLA: What do you mean?

ALANA: It's strange here. I think the walls are talking to me.

ISABELLA: I'm a Wayside Bride.

ALANA: Go on then.

ISABELLA: When I met Hung in nineteen-seventy, there were only about twenty Vietnamese in Australia and they were all Colombo Plan students, sent out by the Vietnamese Government. They all had to enrol in engineering. There was one girl and the rest were young men. Nobody in Australia knew what a Vietnamese person was. Banks didn't even have a form that could fit a three barrelled name. So nearly all of the Vietnamese who were here were Columbo Plan students and Hung and his brothers were almost the only private students. Their father was a businessman and he had six sons and he wanted them out of the country because once you were in the army you had to stay there till you were forty-five. Or dead. He's been vindicated now.

ALANA: With the Fall of Saigon.

ISABELLA: Now Ho Chi Minh City.

ALANA: So if you didn't marry Hung, he would have been sent back to Vietnam?

ISABELLA: Well. Let's just say he was much keener than me on getting married because I wasn't really keen on getting married at all.

ALANA: What was that about?

ISABELLA: That was just me being a girl of my times. It was the early seventies, there was a lot of that stuff going around!

ALANA: What about your family?

ISABELLA: Queenslanders.

They both grimace.

My grandmother was absolutely devastated.

ALANA: That you weren't going to get married?

ISABELLA: That I wasn't going to get married to someone who was white. They thought that would advantage me. My parents wanted me to get married but they certainly didn't have a Vietnamese person in mind.

ALANA: What were your grandmother's objections?

ISABELLA: She was born in eighteen-eighty-two so by nineteen-seventy she was well on in her eighties and all through her life she probably would never have met an Asian person. Most of the Chinese were Australian Chinese, second or third generation, descended from the goldfields. And I was my grandmother's favourite granddaughter so she had high hopes for me.

ALANA: Did you have words?

ISABELLA: She was too old and frail by that stage for a big shouting match but she said that it was the worst moment of her life. That it would be the thing that would kill her.

ALANA: And how did that affect you?

ISABELLA: Oh well, I still remember it vividly. She was otherwise a lovely grandmother.

ALANA: But that was painful?

ISABELLA: Yes. Still is.

Pause.

My parents weren't keen but they knew I was pig-headed and I'd probably end up doing what I wanted to do whatever they said. Hung's Vietnamese family wasn't very keen on the marriage either. In some ways they were even more opposed than mine. They thought, 'Eldest son is lost forever, never going to come back.' But anyway, we went ahead with it.

ALANA: You asked Ted to marry you.

ISABELLA: Hung was a lapsed Buddhist and I was a lapsed Presbyterian. So churches were out. We didn't want a church. And at that stage there were no celebrants. I had been following what Ted was doing at Wayside and I liked the radicalism of Ted's stance. He seemed to be upsetting a lot of people so we thought 'that'll suit us'. We went to a pre-wedding meeting for a chat. I remember he was late for the wedding. Ten or fifteen minutes. It was at Blackburn Gardens, behind the old Woollahra Library. My uncle and my mother and my brother came down.

ALANA: Horrified that you were getting married in a park.

ISABELLA: My mother was absolutely horrified. She didn't think it would be really legitimate, she thought we wouldn't really be married. She was brought up a Methodist and Ted was, nominally at least, a Methodist. So I harped on that point when I was telling her about our plans. I didn't tell her that he was being charged with heresy. Well that was later anyway ... We got married in February nineteen-seventy-three.

ISABELLA *laughs.*

I just said, 'We've got a proper Methodist minister of religion and his name is Ted Noffs'. Which placated her enough to turn up. On the day the sun was shining but she made a point of bringing an umbrella. I designed a lace dress over a crepe underdress to follow the lines of a traditional Vietnamese ao dai. We had lunch at a Chinese restaurant near Cleveland Street then known for its many Labor Party functions and excellent food, and left for Tasmania with a hundred dollars. We had a girl and a boy and are now proud grandparents to our daughter's child. Next year we will have been married fifty years.

SCENE ELEVEN

There is a person cross-dressed in theatrical splendour (as the El Alamein fountain or simply in glamourous glitter) who might hold a sign announcing that we are at The Chevron Hotel Quarter Deck Bar, Kings Cross.

MICHAEL, *a flamboyantly-dressed gay man, sits drinking, holding court with a good-looking sailor.*

MICHAEL: It's like a sixth sense with me, darling. No-one tells me, the US Navy certainly don't publish their arrival schedule, but it's like I can just intuit when a vessel is coming into port. I'll wake up in the morning and throw open the window and I'll think 'Hello Sailor'. Do you know what I mean? No, well of course you don't, darling, you just have to turn up looking all ultramarine and gorgeous. But I can tell you, sweetie, I have a knack for these things. Give me another five minutes and I'll have guessed the exact tonnage of your vessel.

    MARGARET *enters.*

Look out Maryanne, your mother has turned up. Followed you all the way to Sydney to make sure you're not pooncing about with the local poofters.

    MARGARET *walks straight over to* MICHAEL.

SAILOR: You're a long way from Kansas, Dorothy.

MARGARET: He's exactly what I'm looking for.

SAILOR: Well I don't do the missionary position. At least not this early in the day.

    The SAILOR *exits.*

MARGARET: You're the best-dressed man in the room.

MICHAEL: Well spotted.

MARGARET: You have exquisite taste. You have impeccable styling. It is a pleasure to be in the presence of someone so creative and so flawlessly attired.

MICHAEL: Oh, my dear, if all this flattery is in aid of getting me to buy you a drink, consider it done. But otherwise I would ask you to worship me from afar.

MARGARET: I need you to do me a favour.

MICHAEL: My dear lady, I am physiologically unable to render you such a favour.

MARGARET: Not that kind of favour.

MICHAEL: What other sort is worth doing?

MARGARET: I've got a bride in tears, I've got a chapel in chaos, I've got a Minister in despair because the church hierarchy are about the throw the book at him.

MICHAEL: You don't mean Ted?

MARGARET: Yes. Ted Noffs.

MICHAEL: I know Ted. What are they doing to him?

MARGARET: They've declared he's a heretic.

MICHAEL: Happens to the best of us.

MARGARET: No it doesn't. It never happens in Australia.

MICHAEL: I believe the Anglicans charged a Reverend Hayes with heresy in Melbourne in the thirties. He wrote heretical poetry.

MARGARET: I just need you to walk a bride down the aisle.

MICHAEL: Quelle horreur.

MARGARET: As her father, nancy, not as her partner. As a friend of Margaret.

MICHAEL: You mean a friend of Dorothy?

MARGARET: What's Dorothy got that I don't?

MICHAEL: Taste in shoes.

MARGARET: I need a perfectly-dressed man with impeccable manners and a sense of authority. I've got a howling bride and a chapel that's backed up with wedding guests like a cistern backed up with ...

MICHAEL: Alright. I get the picture.

MARGARET: Will you do it?

Pause.

For Ted?

MICHAEL *puts out his hand.*

MICHAEL: Michael.

MARGARET *kisses it.*

MARGARET: Margaret.

MICHAEL: Are they really going to defrock him?

MARGARET: They might.

MICHAEL: It's the other bitches in dresses who will get you every time.

They exit.

SCENE TWELVE

TED: Clyde.

CLYDE DOMINISH *is a Methodist minister. A friend of Ted's.* TED *is very upset.*

CLYDE: Ted. How you going?

TED: No warning, just a notice to appear. No heads up that a charge was being considered.

CLYDE: No warning that they were about to write to you?

TED: Twenty-five years in the ministry, Clyde.

CLYDE: I thought they'd have to give you notice.

TED: They didn't give me notice because they want this. They want to use this new Minister, John Hall, who does not even have his ministerial P plates, they're going to use him to complain about me and get rid of me and shut the place down.

CLYDE: When did the complainant hear you speak?

TED: This young zealot is just the patsy. The hierarchy has got my head in the noose and they're using Hall's complaint to kick the chair out from under me.

CLYDE: We won't let them.

TED: —

CLYDE: Ted?

TED: Tell me why I have to comply with forty-four sermons published by John Wesley in seventeen-fifty-five? The people who come here, what do they care about Methodist canon law? No wait, Methodism doesn't have canon law. Methodism decides who is legitimate on a whim, on a foible, on a hastily typed letter in the post. Wesley preached social involvement. Wesley preached tolerance of divergent views. That's John Wesley the founder of Methodism. If any of these buttocks had the theological chops of John Wesley I would be fine. I don't have the stomach to fight their evangelical piety anymore.

Pause.

TED *is becoming alarmingly unstable, a fear and pain we have not seen previously.*

CLYDE: Any Minister who disputes your legitimacy will have to speak to the discipline committee first, only then can they charge you.

TED: No. No. This is notice to appear before the Committee of Discipline to face a charge of unfaithfulness to the doctrines of the church.

CLYDE: You argue that it's just details, that you still agree with them on the fundamentals.

Pause.

TED: I don't know that I do agree on the fundamentals anymore.

CLYDE: You don't want to leave the church.

TED: Don't I? Maybe I am unfaithful, according to their parameters.

CLYDE: And what about all these people?

TED: They become their problem.

CLYDE: You don't mean that.

Pause.

TED: Don't I? They sit in their plush bloody manses stuffing their faces with scones.

CLYDE: Take a deep breath Ted.

TED: Unfaithful to the doctrines of the church. When they sit in the machinery of an institution that has crushed better men than me, stuffing their faces with ...

CLYDE: Lamingtons.

TED: What?

CLYDE: Reverend Brand likes lamingtons, not scones. Little bits of coconut dropping all down the front of his robe.

TED *laughs.*

TED: Yeah.

CLYDE: We'll fight this Ted. You're not alone.

TED: I'm the only name on the ticket of execution.

CLYDE: Call Jack Hiatt.

TED: Hiatt?

CLYDE: He's a Queens Counsel.

TED: Yeah. I married him to his wife two weeks ago.

CLYDE: Call him.

> *Pause.*

Ted?

TED: So now I have to call a lawyer to defend me against my own people?

CLYDE: They are not your people.

TED: Yes, well I know that now. I'm in no doubt about how little they value me. How easily they think they can do without me. How openly they want to destroy me.

CLYDE: Ted.

TED: Yeah.

CLYDE: Get yourself a lawyer.

SCENE THIRTEEN

MIRIAM, *the bride, enters crying.* TED *goes to her.* MARGARET *enters with* MICHAEL.

MICHAEL: Oh my beautiful darling.

[*Sharply*] You need to stop that this instant.

> *He goes over to* MIRIAM *and puts his arms around her. She looks at him, puzzled.*

MIRIAM: Who are you?

MICHAEL: I'm going to put that remark down to the fact that your eyes are bleary with tears.

MIRIAM: Sorry?

MICHAEL: That's a fine greeting for your old man. And after I've come all the way from ... Where did you grow up?

MIRIAM: Perth.

MICHAEL: And after I've flown in all the way from Perth. You might give your old man a bit of a smile.

TED: Hi, I'm Ted.

MICHAEL: Hello Ted, I'm this beautiful creature's father. [*To* MIRIAM] What is your father's name?

MIRIAM: Rohan.

MICHAEL: Rohan.

He shakes TED*'s hand.*

MIRIAM: But you're not.

MICHAEL: But for you, for today, for the moment, I am.

MICHAEL *winks at her.*

MIRIAM: But, are you okay to pretend?

MICHAEL: My darling, it is what I absolutely do best in the whole widest world. But I will walk out of here right now if you don't stop that crying.

TED: We try to just be with people in their pain, Rohan. We don't try to fix people here.

MICHAEL: That's all very well for reality, Ted, but when it comes to weddings we not only need to stop my beloved daughter from crying, we need to send her down that aisle into the fantasy of her lifetime. We need to help her live …

He gestures with his hand.

… the dream. And it all starts with a debonair, elegant and doting father called Rohan who loves you to bits and insists that your eyes don't look puffy for the photos. Yes?

MIRIAM *nods and smiles.*

MIRIAM: Yes.

MICHEAL: There.

He puts his hand in hers.

MIRIAM: You don't have to love me to bits.

MICHAEL: Miriam, everything else we are pretending, my name, my relationship to you, my unfortunate place of origin. The one thing, the single thing that you can believe is that I do love you.

MIRIAM: But you've only just met me.

MICHAEL: No, my darling. I've known you all my life. You're the one who never gets what they want exactly when they want it. You're the one who hopes so much and loves so deeply but can't make the world notice how special and beautiful you are. You're not Miriam today. You're a bride. In a moment you're the bride. And that vision, that hope and dream, that paean to passion, devotion, amour ... that I absolutely love to bits.

Beat.

So dry those tears and pull yourself up. We're putting on the best show of ourselves we've ever given.

MIRIAM *stands and pats down her dress.* MICHAEL *lifts her face gently under her chin and kisses her on the forehead.*

This is going to be the most ravishing wedding of the year. Yes?

He puts out his elbow for her to hold.

MIRIAM: Thanks for being here, Dad.

MICHAEL: My pleasure.

From the corner the 'witnesses' come forward. ROSIE *puts a bouquet into* MIRIAM*'s hands.*

ROSIE: I know your Mum isn't here but I want to offer you a mother's love, which is my pride in everything that you are.

CLYDE: The words Ted will say to you, they're the same words that have been said again and again over every kind of person and that makes you as equally precious as anyone who has ever been asked them.

MICHAEL *gives* MIRIAM *a paper cup of champagne.*

MICHAEL: The fizz has gone out of the bubbly but it'll still get you happy. That's something to remember after the honeymoon, lovely. Things can go flat but they still taste delicious.

ORSON *puts on* MIRIAM*'s veil.*

ORSON: I couldn't cut the phone lines so ASIO can still hear what you say in there so be careful and don't say anything they can use. I don't want them to see me with you so I won't come in. But go well, Miriam, Diallo loves you.

JOAN: Blood is only one way into love and it's not the only way. Please believe that you are cherished by everyone who is gathered here today.

MIRIAM *looks at* ALANA.

MIRIAM: What about you?

ALANA: Oh, yes. Good on you.

MIRIAM: Good on me? That's a bit common. For a wedding.

ALANA: Top effort.

ROHAN: Here comes the bride.

ALANA: Way to go.

MARGARET: How about we all go into the Chapel?

ALANA: Nice one.

MARGARET: Diallo is waiting for you.

> MIRIAM *nods.*

MIRIAM: Take it away.

TED: We don't actually say 'here comes the bride' you know, Rohan.

MICHAEL: Go with it, Ted, just go with it.

> *They exit,* MIRIAM *and* MICHAEL *processing as if down an aisle all the others following.*

> CLYDE *and* TED *are left onstage.*

CLYDE: Ted. I just called Brand. He's coming to see you.

TED: When?

CLYDE: Today.

TED: Clyde, put him off.

CLYDE: The basis of the charge against you is that you deviate from the theology of John Wesley, the founder of Methodism.

TED: Yeah, and I do.

CLYDE: And so do I. And so, probably, does this young Minister who they're using to bring the charge. John Wesley said women could be preachers in seventeen-sixty-one. So all the practising Methodists who oppose that are in variance.

TED: That's right ... Clyde. That's it. Who's to say?

CLYDE: The penny drops.

TED: Will you, Reverend Brand, as President of the Methodist Conference, discard all of your worldly possessions and lay up nothing more than plain food to eat? If you do not, you yourself are at variance.

> MARGARET *pops back on to get* TED.

CLYDE: Say that. To his face.

TED: Brand is no hardline conservative. He's had his own tussles with the church.

CLYDE: So maybe he's been snookered. And maybe you can convince him not to toe their line.

TED: And if I can't?

CLYDE *puts out his foot.*

CLYDE: Up the wazoo.

Pause. They exit.

ALANA: That's gonna make for a cracker of a second act. Take fifteen.

INTERVAL

Rebecca Massey and Emily Goddard in Belvoir Theatre's Wayside Bride, *2022 (Photo: Brett Boardman)*

ACT TWO

SCENE FOURTEEN

ALANA *is already onstage when* ORSON *enters, accompanied by the sound of many currawongs.*

ORSON: Evergreen mature specimen exotic dense leaves in highly
urbanised
Tree
Significant tree
Smell

> *She lifts her head and smells.*

Sweet bay, heavy magnolia
The green [*very fast grumbling*] stop wanting to change it all the time,
stop it now because I'm scared, I'm scared, [*shouting*] I'm frightened
now of all the changes snap snap snap breaking all the little limbs
Asphalt on the tree, footpath, all the feet on the road
The crime
happens all the time
Currawong
call
into the waiting air
There, there is beauty's newest shape:

> TED *and* MARGARET *enter.* ALANA *is listening from the margins.*

MARGARET: What did Clyde say?

TED: He told me that Brand is coming here. This afternoon.

MARGARET: I've arranged for you to speak to the *Australian* this afternoon.

TED: No. I don't want to take it public.

MARGARET: We need to take it national right from the get go. Murdoch
will run comment too which will flush out your enemies.

TED: Just let me have a crack at him.

MARGARET: At who?

TED: At Brand. I may be able to talk him down.

MARGARET: Ted. He's sent the letter.

TED: Yes but he's coming here so he's open to at least hearing my side.

MARGARET: He's coming here to be able to say that he did.

TED: Let me give him the benefit of the doubt. He knows me. He's not just one of their flunkies. He might listen.

MARGARET: Ted, don't give room to people pretending to be your friend. Talk to Graham Williams at the *Australian* and let him shore up your alliances outside the church.

TED: The church won't back down if I go to the media.

MARGARET: Good. Fuck them.

TED: Margaret!

MARGARET: Sanctimonious boneheads. How dare they.

TED: You're angry.

MARGARET: I'm not angry. I'm absolutely livid, Ted. I have absolutely had it with these holier than thou religious arseholes. If we can get the *Australian* newspaper to lift their cassocks and shove a hot poker up their privates that will be highly satisfactory.

TED: Yes, but it will also be like losing our citizenship. No protection of the Synod, no collaboration with other parishes. And worse, they'll come after these people.

MARGARET: They're already doing that.

TED: They're on the lip of doing it. I need to try to get them to reconsider.

MARGARET: No, you need to go public and use the word heresy every time any journalist asks. They want to play word games we'll give that one enormous word in bold print above the fold. They want to dress up heresy in 'unfaithfulness to the doctrines of the church', well, we'll dress up their corruption in black and blue body blows to the hierarchy of the Methodist Union.

TED: Hell has no fury.

MARGARET: You can't come to the school to see Wes in his end of year play because someone at the Chapel needs you. We can't go on holiday because someone at the Chapel needs you. I haven't been taken out to dinner for my wedding anniversary in ten years because someone at the Chapel needs you. And I haven't complained, I haven't said a word because that's what we needed to do, that's what I married, that's been our mission. But when they call that into question they heap shit on more than you, Ted. I love you, I stand with you Theodore, but when they attack you they attack me, they illegitimate me and my children and all the sacrifices and compromises and endless ways that we have been consumed by this ministry. I have accepted that they don't lift a finger to help us, everyone but the Church has done that, but the day, the day, they start attacking us, through you, that's the day they unlock the Harpy tomb and set a pack of Medusa's maidens onto their heads.

TED: Vengeance is mine, says the Lord.

MARGARET: Yeah, well, with respect Lord, get in line.

They exit.

SCENE FIFTEEN

ALANA *sits alone.* DUSTY *enters and sits down.*

DUSTY: You heard of quid pro ho?

ALANA: I've heard of quid pro quo. A favour for a favour.

DUSTY: Yeah, well, quid pro ho is an explanation for a whore.

ALANA: You call yourself a whore?

DUSTY: Yeah well. Women and men. Prostitution is just degrees, isn't it?

ALANA: —

DUSTY: So what are you about lady? What do you want here? And don't say you don't know.

ALANA *shrugs.*

ALANA: Misery loves company.

DUSTY: What's there to be miserable about?

ALANA: Nothing.

DUSTY: Quid pro ho. It starts when I was sixteen and ran away from home and became a street kid up the Cross. Sexually abused by my older brother. So then I had to fend for myself on the streets. Back in that day the late eighties, early nineties I worked the street because basically I was underaged to work in any parlour or strip club. To learn what to do I just copied the other girls sort of thing. Yeah, and then when I was legally eighteen I worked in the strip clubs. So I've been through everything: the Royal Commission, the nitty gritty, the whole lot of it. I've got a talent when it comes to the street. I can pick a character within ten minutes of conversation.

ALANA: And what do you pick me as?

DUSTY: Curious.

ALANA: Curious strange or curious inquisitive?

DUSTY: I was working the streets for two years. The thing you learn from working. People think that it's one kind of man who comes to sex workers. But it's all walks of life. To me, the way it got drummed into my head to make money is this. It's sideshow alley up here ... Kings Cross ... so if they're dumb enough to give it they're dumb enough to receive it. And the less you give the more they give you. That's the trick with prostitution. A lot of the girls, they're stupid, for fifty dollars, they'll give them a blow job and have sex with them. But if they put that off, they could get much more money, promise them the world and deliver them nothing. That's how you get into the clubs.

ALANA: The sex clubs up and down the main street?

DUSTY: That's right. And my best friend at Striporama was this girl called Sharna.

> SHARNA *enters, they embrace, delightedly.* DUSTY *removes her dressing gown and proceeds to dress and make herself up for work, including a wig.*

SHARNA: I know like it rhymes and is a bit dumb, but we never worked under our real names.

DUSTY: I was called Dusty and she was called Blossom.

SHARNA: Blossom. And I was on with one of the bosses at Striporama.

DUSTY: And I'm on with the other one, Armased. And one night Armased comes back to where we're living and he's really out of it.

SHARNA: And like, this is the kind of thing people can't handle about us girls.

DUSTY: Like because I was raised by parents who were being alcoholics, I have this thing that I really freak out if I'm around someone who's really drunk late at night. Now, I know that sounds weird, being a working girl and a stripper right. But in the club I'm fine. But if I'm at home and Armased comes home drunk, I just like react. And even though I know that's just not what you do with a drunk I get all irrational and that makes him really abusive. And he doesn't hit me or nothing but we just have this big row, right.

SHARNA: So the next day she comes into Striporama, we were about twenty, and she says to Ken, who's the boss I'm on with, 'oh there's this beautiful PVC outfit from Paris, it's got the matching long fuck-me boots and it's got straps on the side and these great gloves.'

DUSTY: They want a thousand dollars, Ken, fifteen hundred with the boots.

SHARNA: And back in that day people didn't have credit card or ATM, everyone walked around with cash, so there was money to be made.

DUSTY: On a bad night you'd make a couple of hundred dollars and on a good night you'd go anywhere past a thousand.

SHARNA: So they've subbed us the money, they subbed me fifteen hundred dollars too, so that we could dance like the Barbie twins.

DUSTY: And we just thought, stuff this.

SHARNA: We went to the airport.

DUSTY: Booked a one way to Perth.

SHARNA: And then we rang them when we got there.

DUSTY: To the hotel.

SHARNA: And said, 'Oh, we're not coming into work.'

DUSTY: So they started screaming,

SHARNA: 'Oh oh, where are you, oh oh.'

SHARNA: So we just say, find us and we hung up.

They laugh.

DUSTY: Two days later they found us.

SHARNA: I don't know how.

DUSTY: They just found us.

SHARNA: They banged on the hotel door and they found us.

DUSTY: And we hadn't been out on the town or so. We were just in the hotel room hibernating, being like idiots.

SHARNA: So I was going out with Ken and I was like getting him back sort of thing as well.

DUSTY: We ended up having to pay the fifteen hundred dollars back.

SHARNA: But it was good while it lasted.

DUSTY: And then because he thought that it was really funny, what we did, Armased asked me to marry him. On my twenty-first birthday, it was a surprise. We went round to the Wayside Chapel and Armased had arranged it all and we signed the papers and then we went into Jay's Hut.

SHARNA: And there were the Tongans, the Samoans, the Comanchero bikers, and the Romanian gangsters who used to own a lot of estates down in Victoria Street.

DUSTY: They put on my wedding party. And there was a ten thousand dollar bar tab at Iguana Bar for me.

SHARNA: The whole of Kings Cross was there, it was insane.

DUSTY: Drugs.

SHARNA: Ecstasy.

DUSTY: Cocaine.

SHARNA: Alcohol

DUSTY: Marijuana.

SHARNA: The whole of the Iguana Bar was closed.

DUSTY: I really appreciated it. A lot of the people who were there, a lot of them aren't here anymore, a few of them are, but a lot of them are either in jail.

SHARNA: Moved on.

DUSTY: Had families.

SHARNA: Got businesses.

DUSTY: Everyone's moved on.

SHARNA: When I was a kid I stole my parents' credit card and when they discovered that they dobbed me in to the police. So then I had to go into juvey and that pretty much fucked me up and so then I came up the Cross.

DUSTY: Like she taught me the ropes because she was more of a street kid.

SHARNA: I got introduced to her and I sort of took her under me wing.

DUSTY: So then I got married and I had two kids. A son, named Tadeo and a daughter called Kacy. And when I wasn't having the kids I was still working. They stopped calling me Dusty and started calling me million dollar baby. In all the years I've been up here, the first eight years I probably would have made a million, easy. And then the rest of it I shot it up my arm. And through all of it, I was losing friends, you know.

SHARNA: We're a tight-knit family up here.

DUSTY: But like some they got bumped off.

SHARNA: Or they died in a car crash.

DUSTY: Going on the nod, and got killed that way.

SHARNA: I had one girlfriend who got squashed to death going in between two cars in Bourke Street.

DUSTY: You know, it's just pathetic.

SHARNA: A car was reverse parking and she was on the nod and she just got squashed.

DUSTY: And we was starting to see many a friend OD as well. That was when they set up the shooting gallery. Like the safe injecting room.

SHARNA: And that idea come from the Wayside Chapel drug programs, they started it way back.

DUSTY: And I just thought, with all that was going on I was gonna go there for my shots. So there was this one time I had a hundred dollar deal and been a pig instead of gettin' a fifty or a seventy. I had it and I dropped and Jake who's one of the big managers there, he's narcaned me and brought me back to life.

> *Pause.*

But Sharna had a brain haemorrhage.

SHARNA: Several brain haemorrhages.

DUSTY: So she dies and leaves four kids behind.

SHARNA: And that was pretty sad and that.

DUSTY: And me and her went through so much when we were kids, you know.

SHARNA: And it hurts me.

DUSTY: But then again I'm glad in a way that she's in a better place.

SHARNA: Because sometimes this place can be hell.

> *Both exit, leaving* ALANA *onstage.*

SCENE SIXTEEN

BRAND *enters wearing a suit.* TED *meets him and they shake hands.*

TED: Welcome.

> MARGARET *has entered behind them.*

MARGARET: Can I get you a cup of tea, Reverend Brand?

BRAND: No thank you, Margaret.

MARGARET: Did you always want to be President of the Methodist Conference?

BRAND: I am humbled by the honour.

> MARG *smiles.*

MARGARET: It's a long way from being called the pinko parson.

BRAND: It's a position of responsibility. I have to uphold the ideals of the Union.

MARGARET: I liked you better when you were Chairman of the Peace Movement.

MARGARET *exits.*

TED: She had to open the letter. It was quite a shock.

BRAND: Yes. For her it must have been.

TED: You might have called. To warn me.

BRAND: I guess we thought you might have expected it.

TED: I didn't expect it.

BRAND: Come on Ted, you've been goading us for some time. The way I see it this is what you've been daring us to do for years.

TED: In what way goading?

BRAND: You know there are people in Methodism who want you gone. You go out of your way to call the church outdated and irrelevant and now you've dragged me into it.

TED: I have no idea what you're talking about. But if you're saying I want this, you're wrong. What I want is to stop this. Together. Here.

TED *hands him the letter.*

Tear it into pieces and let's move on. Let me meet with this Hall fellow and hear him out. Whatever you want. But not this. You don't want this.

BRAND: You published the pamphlet. You wrote the blasphemy. You know we can't ignore it.

TED: All I say in the pamphlet is that that the beginning of faith is doubt.

BRAND: I didn't come to listen to your slogans, Ted.

TED: I said that if you think something is strong enough or true enough then no amount of questioning can weaken it. It either is superior or it isn't. There's no heresy in testing it.

BRAND: You said that it is not Christ's suffering which will save the world but ours.

TED: And that's what I believe.

BRAND: You can believe whatever you want, Ted.

TED: Thank you.

BRAND: You just can't believe it and remain a Methodist Minister.

TED: I can if you say I can.

BRAND: And then everyone starts to get their own ideas of what Methodism is and then what do we have?

TED: We have vibrancy. We have discussion. We have people engaging with faith.

BRAND: We have chaos.

TED: Yes. Glorious, wonderful chaos.

BRAND: And the Union collapses under the weight of dissent and ill-discipline.

Pause.

TED: What can I do? Alan. Tell me and I'll do it.

BRAND: Go through the process. Rap over the knuckles. And stop with the Family of Humanity bullshit.

Pause.

TED: How about you pick up the phone and you say 'Reverend Hall, you're barely out of seminary, why don't you shut up and wait and see what good work Ted Noffs is doing before you cover yourself in bull dung by attacking him.'

BRAND: Because the fact that he is just out of seminary is irrelevant. He sees you baptising children into the Family of Humanity and he asks us how is that part of Methodism. And I don't have an answer.

TED: You could defend me and say that we are all, in some way, at variance but as long as Ted wants to call himself a Methodist, we'll keep him thank you very much.

BRAND: How can I say that?

TED: Shut him down. Don't give him the opportunity to make a name for himself by tearing me down.

BRAND: My hands are tied.

TED *looks at him, realising he cannot shift him.*

TED: You want to get rid of me to appease the conservatives who still doubt you.

BRAND: I do not want to get rid of you.

TED: I don't believe you.

BRAND: Don't you dare try to blame me.

TED: I do blame you.

BRAND: You brought this on yourself. You made your ego more important than your ministry. You are so full of self-importance that you can barely look down on the rest of us from your morally superior mountain.

TED: I'm not doing that.

BRAND: You are. You think you're better than us dumb compliant goons who tick the boxes and stick to the script and agree to the vows we took to love and serve.

TED: You think I don't love and serve?

BRAND: I think you love and serve the people who suit you.

> *Pause.*

TED: Well there it is.

BRAND: There what is?

TED: Your hatred. Your contempt for me.

BRAND: Ted, believe me when I tell you I do not hate you.

TED: Then show me some respect.

BRAND: When have you ever shown me any respect? You'd sooner show respect to a man who is drinking himself to death on the streets.

TED: That man is in honest despair. Whereas you have never been in honest anything.

BRAND: And that's what you need from them, isn't it, Ted?

TED: What?

BRAND: You need them to be helpless and hopeless and dependant on you.

TED: We love them when they can't love themselves.

BRAND: You keep faith from them because if you gave them their own faith then they wouldn't need you.

TED: We love them when their hearts are so broken that they don't dare love themselves.

BRAND: You get distracted by their physical needs when your job is to care for their eternal souls. That's the vow you made to this Church, that's the vow that you are betraying every time you open your mouth.

> TED *punches his hand into the wall so that his hand literally goes through the wall or at least makes a dent in the plaster. It is a thump of frustration, not a threat of violence.*

> MARGARET *runs in.*

MARGARET: Ted. Ted! What are you doing?

TED: Get out.

MARGARET: Reverend Brand I am going to please ask you to respect Reverend Noffs' wishes and please leave.

BRAND: You can't see it, Ted. But you've become a tyrant. You don't have the least amount of humility. You don't have the least amount of respect.

TED: Not for you.

BRAND: No, not for me and not for the church.

TED: Right on both counts. Because a feature of leadership is to defend the margins, to affirm the people of difference. To use the power you have to be the voice that allows for the genius of the fringe position.

BRAND: John Hall would say that he is the fringe and you are the corrupt, cynical centre. You always see yourself as the margin call, what would it do to you to see yourself as the one who has lost his way?

TED: He doesn't understand.

MARGARET: He'll never understand.

Pause. BRAND *goes to leave.*

BRAND: We are saved by grace, Ted. By grace, not by works. So that none of us can boast.

TED: I thought you might look at this place, at the people we are saving.

BRAND: You aren't saving anyone Ted. Only God saves.

MARGARET: Reverend Brand. Please.

BRAND: It will be a committee of your peers.

MARGARET: Is he allowed to have a lawyer present?

BRAND: He won't need one.

MARGARET: Is he allowed to have a lawyer present?

BRAND: I would advise against it. It would be an inflammatory tactic.

MARGARET: That's a yes.

Pause.

BRAND: If the lawyer begins to employ tactics which are deemed not to be in keeping with the theological agenda of the hearing, he will be ejected.

MARGARET: You know that Ted will simply prove that you, that John Hall, that every Minister of the Methodist religion is in some way at variance with the sermons of John Wesley.

BRAND: If he proves that then the matter will be dropped.

TED: The matter will be dropped. But the mud will stick. And then you're hoping my position will become intolerable.

TED *exits.*

BRAND: The hearing will be kept private. I can promise you that.

BRAND *exits.*

MARGARET: Not if I can help it.

MARGARET *exits.*

SCENE SEVENTEEN

ALANA *sits and* PAUL *enters. He addresses* ALANA *resentfully.*

PAUL: You're just looking for kiss jobs, huh?

ALANA: I'm sorry ... ?

PAUL: Do you only want the Pollyanna view of Ted, the one with hearts and flowers?

ALANA: You don't like him?

PAUL: I call him Satan in a safari suit.

ALANA *looks at him with interest.*

ALANA: So give me the juice.

PAUL: Every Sunday my mum's here transcribing the great man's sermons instead being at home with us. Every night I have to sit through boring dinners where she goes on and on about all the people who need her help and how hard up they all are.

ALANA: You resent the time your mother spends at Wayside?

PAUL: Yes. Yes. I do.

ALANA: You want her to stay home and be a good little wife and mother?

PAUL: Her coming here was the beginning of the disintegration of our family.

ALANA: Your mother is a volunteer?

PAUL: Reverend Marilyn Stacy, my mother, has done seven weddings at Wayside. Maybe more. And they're just the ones I remember. She's one of the first female ministers in Australia.

ALANA: You're not proud of your mother?

PAUL: She went from the top of Australian publishing and she just walked away and went into this ... Ministry. And Ted didn't even want her to go to theological college because she's less use to him as a ministerial colleague than as a publisher. I mean she published all of his books. *By What Authority*, she did that.

ALANA: So she had a calling.

PAUL: Yeah, but she also has a family. She's looking out for all them junkies and low lives but if I say that pisses me off I'm the soft tosser who should just suck it up. The kids at my school reckon that Ted, and now Mum, are just attracting the scum in bigger numbers to the Cross. My father is a biochemist and he wouldn't even attend the ordination. He's an atheist and so am I. And I'm not speaking for her, I'm speaking for me. There is always someone at Wayside who has a greater need than me. A life or death crisis. Which they have, every day.

ALANA: But when you're a kid ...

PAUL: When you're a kid you don't give a shit about someone who has a greater need. You just want your mother not to be in danger.

ALANA: You think your mum might be in danger?

PAUL: Bikies reckoned this place was a haven for the beatniks and long hairs so they were dead against the place. Then Ted embraced the bikies and now the place is their home away from home. Parents whose kids have been advised at the crisis centre about drugs, they come here to punch someone's lights out if they disagree with the advice. Ted saying it doesn't matter what religion you are, or if you don't have religion you're still welcome, that gets the religious people's back up. And if Mum's married one of your Catholic parishioners to a Protestant or an Orthodox or a Martian from the planet Zwarb, all of them mob are out there saying Ted and his acolytes are the anti-Christ and the marriage certificates they're handing out aren't worth the paper they're printed on.

ALANA: I'm sure she'll be alright.

PAUL: She's not alright. She's lost it and disappeared into some fever dream about saving the world. It's fuckin' bullshit. Why does it have to be her who takes this on? Why can't somebody else's mother help them get their shit together? But I don't know why I'm telling you. You're not going to put any of this in anyway.

He exits, hurriedly.

SCENE EIGHTEEN

MARGARET *enters, wheeling on a large late seventies designed paper shredder. She hands* ALANA *a pile of pamphlets.*

MARGARET: How about you stay here and shred some pamphlets? Can you do that for me please?

ALANA: Of course.

TED *enters.* MARGARET *nods.* ALANA *begins shredding.*

TED: What are you doing?

MARGARET: I figured if we got rid of all the remaining pamphlets you could deny that he got them from here.

TED: So you think my strategy should be to lie?

MARGARET: No.

ALANA *shreds another pamphlet.*

TED: But you're shredding them anyway.

MARGARET: Yes.

She shreds another one.

TED: Can you stop?

MARGARET: No.

TED: Why?

MARGARET: I like the sound.

TED: You don't worry that it's a waste?

MARGARET: Not at all.

TED: You're really pissed off.

MARGARET: I really am.

She shreds another pamphlet.

TED: Because I blamed you for giving them to him.

MARGARET: Maybe.

TED: I'm sorry I focussed on who gave him the pamphlets.

MARGARET: That's okay.

She shreds another pamphlet.

TED: The pamphlets are not to blame.

MARGARET: I know.

TED: Then stop shredding them.

MARGARET: No.

Pause.

TED: If it wasn't the pamphlet it would be something else.

MARGARET: It wasn't something else.

TED: But it would have been. It always is with these evangelical arseholes.

MARGARET: That's what I think too.

ALANA *shreds another pamphlet.*

TED: What have you done?

MARGARET: I rang Jack Hiatt.

TED: No.

MARGARET: Yes.

TED: I don't need a lawyer.

MARGARET: Reverend Brand just agreed to have you ritually humiliated to make clear that he is the top dog.

TED: Were you listening to that?

MARGARET: The whole street was listening to that.

TED: So charge me.

MARGARET: They're going to.

TED: So bring it on.

MARGARET: The full weight of the Methodist Union.

TED: Just try it and see what you get.

MARGARET: And what will they get?

TED: I'll hit them with more theological chatter than a box full of birds.

MARGARET: You think you can outsmart them?

TED: I know I can. I haven't had these forums and happenings at this place for ten years not to know how to win an argument.

MARGARET: You think you do well in an argument?

TED: You know I do.

MARGARET: You think you can run rings around them?

TED: You know I can.

ALANA *shreds another pamphlet.*

TED: Can you stop doing that?

MARGARET: I asked her to help us.

TED: Then can you ask her now to stop?

MARGARET: Maybe you should make a good argument that she should stop.

TED: A what?

MARGARET: Maybe you should throw yourself on her mercy and see if she stops.

Pause.

TED: Because unless you want it to stop nothing I say makes any difference.

MARGARET: Nothing you can say can stop me.

TED: That's right.

MARGARET: That's right.

TED: Then make your point, Marg. Make your point because I've done four weddings and three pre-wedding meetings, and I've spent the afternoon with a mother who lost her son to drugs, and the people keep coming in waves and waves and waves and now I've got to debate some arrogant fledgling who thinks he can haul me in front of a discipline committee for 'unfaithfulness to the doctrines of the church'.

MARGARET: Because guess what?

TED: What?

MARGARET: He can.

ALANA *shreds another pamphlet.* TED *goes over to the shredder and turns it off at the power point.* TED *is struck with the realisation of his position.*

TED: Nothing I say to the discipline committee will make any difference. Nothing I argue will change their minds. It really is a witch hunt.

MARGARET: I'm glad you've used those words.

TED: Why?

MARGARET: Jack Hiatt, your lawyer who is going to represent you against this complainer, may have whispered into the ear of a *Sydney Morning Herald* journalist who is going to run a story with the headline 'Methodist Minister on Heresy charge'.

TED: When?

MARGARET: Tomorrow morning. Front page.

Pause.

TED: Marg.

MARGARET: Yes, Ted.

TED: Would you consider it presumptuous if I asked if I could embrace you in a gesture of purely human gratitude?

MARGARET: Considering you asked so nicely I think it to be quite appropriate.

TED embraces MARGARET *and kisses her.* ALANA *tries to exit.*

You. Wait.

ALANA *stops.*

TED: [*to* MARGARET] You're very clever.

MARGARET: And that's not all.

Beat.

John Pola is going to take you on as a client.

TED: John Pola. Who is representing ...

MARGARET: I know. Junie Morosi.

TED: Junie Morosi.

MARGARET: I know. Do you think we might get to meet her?

TED: Junie Morosi. Who is in a ...

MARGARET: Sexual liasion. I know.

TED: With the Deputy Prime Minister ...

MARGARET: Jim Cairns. I know.

TED: He is married and she's ...

MARGARET: I know. Pola will only have two clients. A witch and a heretic!

MARGARET *tears a pamphlet up with her hands and throws them into the air as confetti.*

TED: John Pola, the PR man. On my side. They won't know what's hit them.

MARGARET: And a group of alcoholics are going to jump on a train to the Central Coast and camp outside Hall's church.

TED: What?

MARGARET: Big mob of pissed off piss-pots are going to sleep rough in the grounds of the church of the Minister who complained about you.

TED: Yeah, maybe don't call them piss-pots.

MARGARET: Okay but did I make up for giving that Minister a pamphlet?

Pause. TED *smiles.*

TED: I thought you were supposed to reign in my impulsive side?

MARGARET: Reign in your own impulsive side, mate. I'm not your mother.

TED: So who are you, Marg?

MARGARET: I'm your wife. I have a certificate that says so.

TED: Dazed, confused and just trying to make it through the day.

MARGARET: Hanging on to stability with the tips of my fingernails.

TED: No you're not. You know exactly who you are.

> TED *lapses into a deep, painful silence.*

ALANA: They're just jealous, you know.

> TED *nods. He and* MARGARET *begin picking up all the torn-up pamphlets.*

They're jealous of your freedom.

TED: Yep.

ALANA: And they're jealous because you're right.

TED: I know.

MARGARET: People in power hate the one who the community makes their leader because the powerful can't control it. It's the one thing they absolutely detest. Because they take power. But when the people of the Cross, the young, the defeated ... the druggies, the crims ...

TED: I don't call them that.

MARGARET: Every time they try to crush you the people see it and make you stronger.

TED: I know.

MARGARET: Then what's wrong, Ted. What's wrong?

TED: They really are that petty.

MARGARET: Unfortunately they are.

TED: But if they claimed me. If they could see what I'm doing and do it ...

MARGARET: They're not going to do that.

TED: As he was leaving, I said to Brand, 'Didn't Jesus say suffer the little children unto me? And he snapped at me, 'Leave Jesus out of this.'

MARGARET: What a numbskull.

> MARGARET *and* TED *burst into laughter. Once they start they can't stop. They are really laughing now. Howling with laughter. Infectiously laughing.*

And now I'm going home.

TED: Yep.

MARGARET: How long are you going to be?

TED: I'll be right behind you.

> MARGARET *begins to exit, when* BILL CREWS *enters suddenly.*

MARGARET: Bill Crews.

> *She continues to exit.*

Tell them about the brotherhood.

SCENE NINETEEN

BILL CREWS: That's what Margaret called the church. The brotherhood. Actually she called it the bloody brotherhood. When I started at Wayside I was running the crisis centre and the social work programs. And. Look. The church is an institution like a bank or anything else. A lot of people who get into the hierarchy are not ... entirely competent. So Ted went round them, and ignored them. And the strain of doing that is ... enormous.

One my first memories of Ted is in a white suit with white shoes. Ted wasn't a great teacher, but if you watched you could learn. So I watched. And in the beginning I thought 'Once I'm ordained, if I do everything opposite to Ted I'll be alright'. But I've found that it's just the same. I used to think, maybe if I'm not so, you know Ted would travel his own path. I thought if I try to go along with people. But it doesn't matter. I still got into trouble. In the end people in the institution sell their souls to the institution. And so if you don't they never trust you. They never trust you.

> *Pause.*

A lot of people did support Ted. John Singleton. Dick Smith. Norman Tieck, who founded the Franklins food chain. Don Chipp. Billy McMahon used to come and talk a lot. Gough Whitlam. Jack Mundey, you'd get the whole plethora and half of them Ted had married. Johnny O'Keefe, he married Johnny. Ita Buttrose.

When you marry two people ... it's ... you'll be standing beside the groom and the bride will appear. And that moment the guy will look at her and ... it's just sheer magic. Like it doesn't last but that moment it is magic. The weddings and baptisms and the funerals, the crisis times in people's lives ... you get to see in their souls.

And the weddings we were doing ... it was people who loved their partner so much that they were willing to go against society to marry them. That's real love. Real love. You see it today with the gay weddings. And it's disgraceful that the church still won't do that. Disgraceful. I've had to have security guards at weddings, against former spouses. I've had parents come and try to stop the wedding. I think life is pretty grey for a lot of people and a wedding is a moment of sunshine and to be part of that is a real blessing and it gives you strength to deal with the misery.

Ted said I'm going to go my own way and bugger the institution. And the cost of that is intense loneliness.

You see it with every whistle-blower.

You see the best in people and the absolute worst.

Yeah, if you want to find love you find it in individuals not in institutions. I remember I was with him one day in his office ... and it was in the middle of the heresy trial and he was quoting all this biblical stuff and he was furious, uptight, trying to let the energy out...

BILL *starts crying. Momentarily can't go on.*

I got hauled in front of all the authorities for that statue in memory of the Korean comfort women. They told me to take it down and I thought. Bugger 'em. But you get one after the other after the other coming at you.

The thing I learned from Ted was to get protection and support outside of the institution. The first thing I did when I set up Exodus was contact the newspapers. You have to watch your back all the time. But the worst thing is the loneliness.

SCENE TWENTY

TED *is standing onstage when* ORSON *rushes over to him.*

ORSON: Ted.
TED: Orson.
ORSON: I see. I hear.
TED: Do you?
ORSON: You too.
TED: Not really. Sort of.

ORSON: You know the phones at the Chapel are tapped. They police are tapping the phones.

TED: I wouldn't be surprised if they do actually.

ORSON: Yeah, they do. Because, you know ... who Miriam married today ...

TED: Diallo.

ORSON: Diallo was a radical student leader at the University of Western Cape. He was detained and banned under the suppression of communism act.

TED: Really?

ORSON: He managed to escape and stowed away on a ship for Australia. The immigration department were looking for him.

TED: But now they can't detain him.

ORSON: Not now you've married them.

> ORSON *looks at* TED.

Would you have still married them?

TED: Of course Orson, of course I would.

ORSON: You would have too, I know you, you would have.

TED: Orson, thank you for trusting me with that.

ORSON: I lost my little baby, you know.

TED: Did you?

ORSON: Yeah. He died. And the Anglicans, they wouldn't bury him. Because he wasn't baptised. I took his ashes and I scattered them around the base of the Magnolia tree. Yeah. And now I see him in the flowers, I hear him in the birds. He was folded up in me but now he's not folded anymore.

> *Beat.*

Is he?

TED: No. I'm sure he's not.

> ORSON *looks around nervously.*

ORSON: Shhhhh. Shhhhh.

TED: What?

ORSON: Shh.

> ORSON *shuffles off. The shadows of the bull bay magnolia play on the walls and across* TED'*s face.*

SCENE TWENTY-ONE

JOSEPHINE *enters. She leans against the wall and then slides down it, semi-slumping on the ground.* ALANA *enters. She walks past* JOSEPHINE, *then realising she is in trouble, goes over to her.*

ALANA: Josephine?
JOSEPHINE: Wha?
ALANA: It's me.
JOSEPHINE: Yeah.
ALANA: Are you alright?
JOSEPHINE: Le me 'lone'.
ALANA: Let me help you try to get up.
JOSEPHINE: Piss off.

> *She roughly pushes* ALANA *back.*

ALANA: What's happened to you?
JOSEPHINE: Gravity.
ALANA: I can't just leave you here.
JOSEPHINE: You got what you come for.
ALANA: What?
JOSEPHINE: You got ... only thing I've got to give ya. An' I give it to ya 'ere.

> *She puts her hands on her shoulders and then her hands in a push in the air, mimicking giving something to* ALANA.

ALANA: Have what?
JOSEPHINE: My story. My story that's the only thing that's still mine.

> *She starts to cry and slumps again to the ground.*

ALANA: Come on. Please, Josephine. You can come with me.
JOSEPHINE: Don't bother.
ALANA: Of course I'll bother.
JOSEPHINE: Don't bother. I'm nothing. Nothing. I not worth nothin' to nobody.
ALANA: Since when?
JOSEPHINE: She didn't leave me.
ALANA: What?

JOSPEHINE: That's just what they told me. And I went and believed them, didn't I? The lie. She never left me, they stole me. They stole me and a whole generation. And now I don't know what is true. Maybe I just don't want to believe she left me or maybe I can't believe that there are people in the world who can deliberately separate a little baby from her own mother.

She lets out a howl of pain. JOSEPHINE *takes her hand.*

I made you welcome, didn't I?

ALANA: You did, you welcomed me.

JOSEPHINE: Tell me.

ALANA: I was all alone. Fish out of water. And you spoke to me. You looked in and you spoke to me, and you were the first. Apart from Orson. But she wasn't exactly speaking to me.

JOSEPHINE: I'm full of shit, you know. You should scrape me off the bottom of your shoe while you still can.

ALANA: Yeah, well, if my brains were shit, Josephine, I wouldn't have enough to fart.

JOSEPHINE: Don't know shit from clay, huh?

ALANA: So stupid I'd eat a shit sandwich …

ALANA *and* JOSEPHINE: … only I don't like bread.

JOSEPHINE *laughs.*

JOSEPHINE: I remember you, you the funny one.

ALANA: Yeah, Josie, that's me. I'm the funny one.

JOSEPHINE: I don't need you to solve me. Solve ye fucking self.

ALANA: You solve yer self.

JOSEPHINE: Not until you solve yourself first.

ALANA: That's not likely any time soon.

JOSEPHINE: No, I don't reckon it is neither.

ALANA *removes the* JANICE *hairband or wig and sits, reflecting.*

SCENE TWENTY-TWO

The sound of the Quarterdeck Bar. A popular song from 1975 plays as TED *enters.*

MICHAEL: Bit late for another wedding, isn't it, Rev?

TED: I just came to say thank you for today.

MICHAEL: Oh well, I'd say anytime but I know you'd never let me forget it.

TED: Nah, but don't be a stranger if you'd like to come say hello, Rohan.

MICHAEL: Michael.

TED: Of course. Rohan is your adopted name.

MICHAEL: My stage name.

> *They laugh.*

Will you stay for a drink?

TED: It's been a long day.

MICHAEL: For a new friend of the family?

> *Pause. He nods. The* GLAMOROUS DRAG PERSON *enters with drinks on a tray.*

TED: Soda water thanks.

MICHAEL: Tea total?

TED: Just need to keep my wits about me.

MICHAEL: You expecting we might be raided?

TED: Lord, I hope not.

MICHAEL: That's the first time I've heard you call on your God. Wasn't much of that in the service today.

TED: No, there isn't usually. Most people don't want it and if they do they can go elsewhere. That's not what I'm about.

> *They clink glasses.*

MICHAEL: Bottoms up.

TED: I hope that doesn't have a double-entendre attached.

MICHAEL: Dear Ted, the only thing I've got an attachment to is the hope of leaving these premises with a good-looking man on my arm.

TED: In a wink or straightaway?

MICHAEL: How do you know about that?

TED: A young man named Aaron, who used to work up on the Wall, the wall of the old Darlinghurst jail up on Burton Street. He used to tell me that a lot of his clients were married men and he'd call them mister straightaway and the camps he'd call 'in a wink'.

MICHAEL: A dink in a wink.

TED: Something like that.

MICHAEL: You are well informed.

TED: I go up there sometimes too, just to talk to the boys, see what they need. Clean clothes, hot meal, they tell us what they need.

MICHAEL: What happened to Aaron?

TED: Disappeared. Like so many of them. You hope they've got out in a good way but you know that mostly they've just gone out. Either way I'll never know.

MICHAEL: And doesn't that pull you down sometimes?

TED *is silent. And then slowly, unexpectedly, he begins to cry.*

TED: What pulls me down, Michael, is a petty group of religious zealots who have the pompous arse to haul me into their bible study antics while young men are being murdered. Who would rather hide behind their traditions while the lives of their neighbours are being destroyed. And they have the presumption to make me answer technical questions about how many angels can dance on the head of a bloody pin.

MICHAEL: Who's making you answer questions?

TED: No-one. Nothing. It's nothing. I mean you might see something on the front page of the paper tomorrow. But trust me, it's flotsam. Rubbish. Not compared to what you people go through every day of your life. Every day, scared you'll be jailed just for being who you are.

MICHAEL: South Australia have decriminalised homosexual acts. I know it took a gay academic being thrown in the river by the South Australian police. But hey, you're part of a religion that says someone always has to die, doesn't it? That there always has to be the sacrificial lamb?

TED: Not for much longer.

MICHAEL: Not for much longer the lamb, or not for much longer part of the religion?

TED *wipes his eyes. Composes himself.*

TED: Thanks for the drink, Michael. I hope you won't be a stranger.

He gets up to leave.

MICHAEL: They do give them such dreadful haircuts, the police, it's no wonder they're all so terribly cranky.

TED: I think the recent crop of Methodist Ministers must be going to the same barbers.

MICHAEL: Could be.

TED: Sorry 'bout the tears. Big day.

MICHAEL: If you can't let it out with a queen, who can you let it out with?

TED: Me, usually.

MICHAEL: Even saints need a little sob now and then.

TED: I'm no saint.

MICHAEL: Aim high, Ted. Don't settle for mere martyr.

TED: Yeah. Right.

MICHAEL: You can't go without having a dance.

TED: Yes, I can.

MICHAEL: No, come on. One dance, it's not a waltz. There's no physical contact.

They get up. The music gets loud.

MICHAEL and TED dance. TED is appropriately awkward. Now the stage fills with all the characters from the past: DUSTY and SHARNA, MARGARET and JOSEPHINE, ORSON and the DRAG QUEEN and CLYDE, all dancing and swirling through time and space.

During the dance at some point TED sinks to his knees, face in his hands, crippled with the pain of what he is going through.

MICHAEL helps him up. He hugs TED and exits.

SCENE TWENTY-THREE

TED *turns to exit. But* ALANA *stops him.*

ALANA: Ted.

TED: Yes.

ALANA: I'm Alana. I'm the playwright.

TED: Oh, hello.

ALANA: I must have come in the wrong entrance.

TED: No I think I was supposed to exit that side.

ALANA: No, that's good. Otherwise I wouldn't have met you.

TED: Very nice to meet you.

ALANA: Actually I did meet you. I was eight. You married my mother. To my stepfather. I found the dress she wore to your pre-wedding chat.

TED: Divorcee?

ALANA: Yes.

TED: How is your mother?

ALANA: Oh she died, twenty years ago.

TED: You must have been young.

Pause.

ALANA: I've got to get to the next scene, Ted.

Beat.

I rather indulgently offered myself up as a metaphor.

TED *stops her.*

TED: All through my time at the Chapel, all through the years, I met so many people who had a story, had a unique wonderful story. But they didn't know how to ... how can I put this ... they didn't know how to tell it. They could tell me bits and pieces about what went wrong and the choices and the circumstances. But left to make sense of it all in one coherent ... line ... they couldn't. And they were the people who came to the Chapel. They had all the feelings and all the rebellion but they couldn't make sense of it. And I loved those people and I loved helping them find and tell and know the story of their lives. Isn't that what you want to do?

ALANA: Of course.

TED: Then let it be random and chaotic and full of grimy glamour. I was never so much myself, Alana, as when I was being onside with ... someone else.

ALANA: What do you mean?

TED *sets up two chairs for he and* ALANA *to sit in.*

TED: Some people forgive themselves and empathise with their own story only when they're seeing it through someone else's eyes.

ALANA: But why is that?

TED: Something taught them that they're not worthy of that sort of respect. But they are.

Pause.

TED: You conjured all this up. And now, here I am. What do you want to say to me?

Pause.

ALANA: Nothing special. I'm not unique or especially ... special in any way.

TED: But ...

ALANA: [*in a small voice*] But all my life I have been subject to the hatred of religion. Am still subject to it. Whether the law changes a little or a lot, there are so many of us that the institution has crushed with hatred and self-hatred. Lonely little earnest girls who are told they are evil, beautiful broken men who are rejected and humiliated by the superiority of the religious.

TED: I carved out a little place in the madness for the dreamers and the trauma survivors to ask questions and find love.

ALANA: —

TED: Do not cling to me, but go.

ALANA: What?

TED: Nothing like that was present
Nothing like that was there
Nothing but the wanderer's lostness
Nothing but silent despair.

TED *exits.*

SCENE TWENTY-FOUR

JANICE *enters.*

JANICE: It was a shame that he had his stroke young, died too soon. They acquitted him of that first heresy charge, you know, but that wasn't the only time. There were two other official investigations. He beat them back three times but I think it broke him. Well. They do, don't they? A lot of it's changed now, of course. Well, some of it

has. I think it's changed less than people think. The same minister of
religion who could refuse to marry me can still refuse to marry you.

ALANA: But one day, one day even that will change.

JANICE: Yeah. I hope so. In any case that was a credible stab at my day
by the Wayside.

ALANA: Thank you.

JANICE: All I did was sit and listen, it's nothing.

ALANA: That's pretty much all I do, too.

JANICE: Well, I guess that's where you get it from then.

ALANA: It wasn't just because it was around the corner.

> JANICE *shakes her head.*

It was because you fitted.

> *Beat.*

You died too young, Mum.

JANICE: Yeah.

> *Beat.*

But I left you my sewing machine.

ALANA: The one with the magic thread.

JANICE: All you need in life is tension in your bobbin.

> *Pause.*

Do you remember anything of that day? That day I was married at
Wayside?

ALANA: Fragments. Moments. Nothing that adds up to a story.

JANICE: Like what?

ALANA: I remember a little girl with bare legs and knobbly, scarred knees.
In the photo she's clutching a long-handled, white handbag with her
white-gloved hands and looking at the camera, bewildered. In the
photograph is her mother and grandmother, both now dead. She looks
at her beautiful, tiny-waisted mother and wishes that she could ask
her about that day. That day, at least, when her mother looked happy.

I remember being in your bedroom, watching you place the tiny
white silk daisies in nooks of the bee-hived wig on a foam mannequin
head. I remember you secured the lapels of your wedding outfit with
anchor-embossed silver buttons, because you were marrying a sailor.

JANICE *exits.*

I held that photograph in my hand and I made a vow — to mine the living for the story of what Australian religious rebellion looks like. I went looking for Wayside brides, and their grooms, and I caught the held breath of people who were the alternatives, and the edges, and the discarded and the different — I caught the sharp intake of breath of my own curious, long-dead mother who gave me the gift of life.

And now there's just one more thing I need you to stay and witness.

Suddenly JON OWEN *enters.*

JON: Hi, I'm Jon Owen.

ALANA: Jon, welcome.

JON: I'm going to conduct the ceremony.

ALANA: Great. And now if this works how it's supposed to …

CLAIRE *and* JOANNE *enter.*

CLAIRE: Hi, I'm Claire, I'm a Wayside bride.

JOANNE: And I'm Joanne. I'm a Wayside bride. Too.

JON: Nice shorts Joanne.

IRMA *enters, wearing a beanie.*

CLAIRE: We were going to bring a camera. An actual camera, not our phones. But Joanne got angry about all these cords being around.

JOANNE: So I threw the camera cord out so we couldn't charge it.

CLAIRE: And I got really cranky and I think when I get nervous I pick a fight.

JOANNE: You do.

JON: Well you're here now. And I think Irma will shoot a video if you'd like that.

CLAIRE: That would be wonderful, thank you, Irma.

IRMA: But neither of you have a bouquet.

CLAIRE: No. Do we need one?

IRMA: Of course.

JOANNE: Not for me.

IRMA *exits as* CHARLIE *enters playing the guitar.*

JON: So, Joanne, you have any music planned? We can hook up your phone. Or Charlie can play the guitar.

JOANNE: Charlie, for sure.

CHARLIE: I'm a bit overdressed.

CLAIRE: You look brilliant.

CHARLIE: I'll play as you walk down the aisle.

CLAIRE: We weren't planning on walking ...

JON: You don't have to walk down the aisle.

CHARLIE: But at least from one end of the rooftop garden to the other.

CLAIRE: Don't you keep bees over there?

CHARLIE: Native bees.

JON: The brides walk through a swarm of bees and we say that prepares them for married life.

CHARLIE: Most places you get confetti, Wayside you get native bees.

IRMA returns with some lavender in a simple but lovely bouquet. MARGARET and TED are with her, dressed as Wayside street people.

IRMA: Your bouquet.

CHARLIE begins to play a very slow acoustic guitar.

CLAIRE: Who will walk with us?

ALANA: Margaret.

CLAIRE: Noffs?

ALANA: No. Her namesake. The actor Maggie Blinco.

MAGGIE enters.

MAGGIE: Short for Margaret.

CLAIRE: Honoured to have you here Maggie.

MAGGIE takes CLAIRE's arm. ALANA takes JOANNE's arm. MARGARET and CLAIRE and ALANA and JOANNE walk across the stage to JON, CLAIRE holding flowers, CHARLIE playing the guitar, IRMA capturing it on video. CLAIRE hands the bouquet to ALANA and JON binds the hands of CLAIRE and JOANNE with his stole.

JON: Do you, Joanne, wish to be married to Claire, and to cherish the love and commitment that you make to each other on this day?

JOANNE: I do.

JON: And do you Claire, wish to be married to Joanne and to cherish the love and commitment that you make to each other on this day?

CLAIRE: I do.

JON: In the presence of these witnesses, and by the power vested in me by the Commonwealth of Australia, I join these two people in holy matrimony and I pronounce you to be legally and officially two married persons.

JOANNE *kisses* CLAIRE.

There is an explosion of confetti and music.

The cast turn and bow.

THE END